Hripsime

by

J. Barrie Paulson

PublishAmerica
Baltimore

ISBN: 1-4241-6602-0
PUBLISHED BY PUBLISHAMERICA, LLLP
www.publishamerica.com
Baltimore

Dedication

This book is dedicated to Hripsime's daughter, Marie Badeer and her family, and to her siblings and their families. Marie, a very good friend to my mother, Dorothy Johnson, and to me is truly an anointed teacher of the Bible, who has inspired and touched the hearts of many throughout the years in Omaha, Nebraska, in the USA.

Acknowledgement

This story is a derivation from Hripsime M. Kassarjian's Autobiography
Survived: How and Why?

Although several years had passed since I first read Hripsime's story, I never forgot it. Hence, when 9-11 transpired, I decided to write my version of this most extraordinary Christian woman's story, as I felt most ardently it should be shared with everyone.

In the preface of her little book is the following prayer:

"My prayer for each and everyone of you who by reading the wonderful miracle-working power of Almighty God, may grow in solid faith in Him, with whom nothing is impossible, in different, hopeless situations, in single and in family life as well. May God's rich blessings be upon each one of you.
With much love and prayer in Christ Jesus."

Hripsime M. Kassarjian
(Unknown—January 1985)

Preface

Hripsime, named after the daughter of an Armenian king, a princess and a beautiful young girl of eighteen years, became a Christian toward the end of the Third Century A.D.

There was a prince, the son of a gentile king, who intended to marry her if she would give up her faith in Jesus Christ. He tried to persuade her for some time, but without any result, so he put her in jail. Everyday this prince would visit her to find out if she had changed her mind, but her answer was always the same. She would tell him, "It is far better to die for my dear Savior, Jesus Christ, than to marry a gentile prince." When she finally died in jail, the people called her a saint.

Hripsime never felt she was worthy to bear this princess's name, but many believing parents named their daughters in memory of this dear princess, who had held fast to her faith and to her deep abiding love in Jesus Christ.

– One –

A set of nervous footsteps paced outside her door and then a sharp, rhythmic knock cut into all consideration. At the kitchen sink, with her hands in warm dishwater, Hripsime turned her head, but without missing a beat with what she was doing.

"Come in," she said, confident as to whom it was.

"It is coming, Hripsime. It is coming very soon," said her next-door neighbor in a high, shrill, trembling voice.

The door swung open and she rushed in leaving it ajar. Running to the sliding-glass door that led to Hripsime's little balcony, impatiently, her brow moved up and down as her frantic eyes looked into the sky and then into the street below. Her head bobbed back and forth as fast as her feet. Not once did she look at Hripsime to see what she might be doing. The expectation was that all should stop for what was now being said or done.

"What's coming?" Hripsime said calmly, as she placed the remaining plates in the rack next to the dishpan. She did not know why she had posed such a question, as she knew the answer well enough.

"The war! The war is coming! What will we do, Hripsime? They want to kill us all," she cried out in much anguish finally glancing Hripsime's way.

Again her neighbor turned to look at the sky and then to the street below. Then she scurried to the open door that led to the hall. Wildly she fingered the doorknob, first looking at Hripsime, then at the glass door to the balcony, and then back to Hripsime. Hripsime knew that her neighbor was speaking the truth, but did not want to add to her frightened tears.

"We will be fine. God will bring us through this," Hripsime said, with much assurance.

"I must go and tell the others," her neighbor bawled, with tears that streamed down her cheeks like two rivulets. Her hands twisted within one another as if she were grinding something to a pulp. It was as if Hripsime had never spoken; her neighbor's fears seemed to totally consume her.

When the door slammed, Hripsime listened as her neighbor's heavy footsteps, as she headed downward onto the landing and then down to the next floor below. Again, she heard knocking, but now the rapping was distant and not as penetrating. Then more excited voices joined in with her neighbor's agitated timbre. More doors were opening and shutting and there was much clamorous chatter and alarm. This repetitive outringing of annoying sounds kept Hripsime's mind busy for several minutes, but then the frantic footsteps dissipated as they continued on down into the lower regions of the building. After a short time, the only sound was muffled voices and soft weeping.

Hripsime looked down into the soapy water at her hands that lay flat-palmed as if they were stuck to the bottom of the dishpan. As she wiggled her fingers, she watched the motion of the water. It reminded her of a stormy, foamy sea and of the manmade storm that soon would be upon them. The black clouds that had been accumulating over Beirut were now ominous, fuming, rolling thunder claps with fully armed lightening bolts that resembled drawn swords. Held in check until they could come clashing down on 1975 Beirut and the Christian Quarter, she was sure these war-like bolts would be the most destructive blows possible.

Suddenly, all in one swift motion, she wielded her hands up out of the water, caught a dishtowel that hung on a hook by the sink, and turned to look out at the small balcony of her fourth-floor flat. After hanging the towel neatly back on its hook, she strolled toward the glass door. Again, she wiped her hands on the skirt of her pinafore-style apron that wrapped around her body. She held the hem in her fingertips; they felt clammy and not dry enough. While tucking a few strands of her gray-white hair into the braids that crisscrossed the top of her head like a crown, she stood at the glass door briefly before sliding it to one side. Watching the glare of her image wave across the glass, she straightened her apron as she stepped out onto the balcony.

A slight breeze brushed against her face and loosened a few strands of hair that softly caressed her cheeks and neck. Her dark eyes scanned all things below and beyond. She could taste the salt of the sea, as she extended her vision across the rooftops of her beloved Beirut, past the line of resort hotels along the beach, and then across the shoreline until they rested on the marina where many fishing and pleasure boats resided. Then she watched the sea gulls that dotted the water's edge and maneuvered themselves in and out around the boats.

Across the great watery expanse, shimmering from the heat of the day, she looked on at the dramatic long line of the horizon that divided a yellow sky from the blue-green Mediterranean. Captivating much of the heavens was a massive burning sphere. The sea seemed ablaze when it touched the edge of the water. Its image created a pathway across the water to the city. Gradually, the blood red, boiling ball was slipping below the surface. Then only half of it could be seen, then only the top edge, and then it was gone. Again, she became aware of the salty breeze. Refreshingly, it caressed her thoughts.

Leaving the door open, Hripsime casually stepped back inside and sank down into the seat of a straight-back chair. An empty feeling now came over her, as she fingered the white, linen tablecloth that covered the small kitchen table. Still scanning what was outside, she thought about her husband of many years past. Eight years had now passed since he had gone home with his Lord.

Oh, how I miss you, my sweet husband, she whispered. *It seems like it was only yesterday you left me. Oh, how time flies. If you were only here now,* she thought almost aloud. *You were always such a comfort. Your no-nonsense faith, it bolstered me beyond such fears as I now feel. Oh, I miss you terribly, my dear one.*

Then her fingers reached for her Bible that was at the other end of the table as it always was. Its scuffed exterior and ruffled, dog-eared pages showed excessive wear, but she would never trade it for a new one. Then something distracted her. A commotion below in the street was steadily intensifying and its abrasive noisiness fully interrupted her thoughts. Again, Hripsime arose and ventured to the railing of her balcony. Looking down, she watched as the people were spilling wildly into the streets. She knew the routine. She had seen it all before, maybe not here but elsewhere. Everybody was running to buy food because soon the shops would close and they would not be open for how long no one knew, only God.

As she watched the to and fro confusion, it heightened her remembrances of the horrors of previous wars she had endured. Suddenly, she felt laden with the weight of the world as she thought about what this war entailed. The whole target of the enemy was this sector of Beirut, the Christian Quarter. Some Jews were intermingled among the Christians, but most were church-going believers. This was another grand opportunity for the Muslims and new leftists, that had recently converged upon the city, to do away with the infidel, the Christian or Jew or anyone that might be related to their cause. Along with all other conflicts, the whole of the plan was to kill, burn, and destroy, to demolish the entire area, to turn it into a heap of ashes. This was all anyone had talked about these past few weeks and she knew this same shocking talk waved through the whole of Lebanon. Then it seemed she could not adjust her thinking to anything but her memories of long ago.

Hripsime tried to recall the images of her parents; however, this was hard as she was very young the last time she saw them. Still, the memories of her mother's warm loving embrace and her father's soft voice as he bounced her on his knee easily rekindled her imagination. What held fast in her memory was that they prayed on every occasion, read the Bible daily, and sang praises to the Lord each Sunday with beautiful angelic-like voices.

Born an Armenian, into a Christian, Protestant home in Zeitoun, Turkey, in the Taurus Mountains, Hripsime began to recall the little village of her childhood years. Seemingly, it was a peaceful existence and life was conceivably prosperous with many happy times and many relatives. Besides her parents and her younger brother, there were many aunts, uncles, cousins, nieces and nephews.

Situated on the slope of a mountain, Zeitoun boasted of its fruit and vegetable gardens and its vineyards. The grapes of Zeitoun were of the best kind. The houses were built in such a way that the roof of one house was the balcony of the next. And if a person stood back away from it any distance, they looked like stair steps that climbed from the bottom to the summit. In the summertime, most families would move to the high mountains to summer homes to tend their gardens and vineyards. With no machinery, the hard work was all done by hand. Her father was an expert beekeeper as well. He maintained fifty hives, which were always full of bees and oozed with much honey.

Hripsime's parents would often tell her of her first years and how they feared the arrival of their fourth child, that three sisters had preceded her, and all had died in infancy. And, so they coddled Hripsime as if she were a china doll. For months, her mother never took her beautiful, lovely baby out from the house, but then something happened that no one could control. The worst epidemic of small pox ran rampant through their little village on the hillside. Perilously it spread throughout the community and many babies died or many lost the sight of one or both of their eyes. No medicines or vaccinations were attainable. Only home remedies were available and these had no real effect on small pox.

Sadly, the dreaded disease struck Hripsime and her parents felt there was no hope for her survival. Not able to take her mother's milk, for three days, she could not open her eyes. Her father and mother became very depressed. Crying out to God for help, they lit two candles, placing one at her head and the other at her feet, fully expecting her to die. Then a miracle occurred. God healed Hripsime and also saved her eyes.

As Hripsime tried to recall her childhood, small happenings began to trickle into her mind. A big remembrance was the weather; the winters in Zeitoun were very severe. Always many meters of snow covered the ground and no one could go out during a snowstorm. Afterwards, a few brave young men would open a path with shovels, but only a small pathway enough for only one person was ever accomplished. Her father would seat her younger brother on his back and then hold her hand as they walked to the little schoolhouse along the path of the narrow curving, towering drifts.

The little schoolhouse, a very primitive building, had a wood-burning stove in the middle of the room. A narrow carpet made of goat's hair ran along the four walls. This was where they all sat on their knees while they read and wrote their lessons. Shoes lined the entryway. Some mornings Hripsime would carry a piece of wood, as the teacher would permit these children to sit nearest the stove. Her feet were always soaking wet, as it was for all the children; no one had boots to protect their feet. She now reminisced about how she would wiggle her toes to regain some feeling in them, and she remembered well the warmth of the fire upon her feet.

Hripsime was never sure of her age. During these times, families never celebrated birthdays. However, she thought her age might have been six or seven years when she lost her entire family: her father and mother, two married sisters with their families, and her younger brother. Also lost was everything they owned: the two houses, the gardens, the lush vineyards and the fifty beehives.

Under Turkish rule, the Turks considered all Armenians, as "thorns-in-their-sides," and the people of the little village of Zeitoun were no exception. Her father would tell of the bravery and courage of the men and women of their village. They had fought off the "Young Turks," a new and more aggressive movement that began in the late 1870s, thirty-nine times, defeating them every time. However, before the last battle, the Turks found a way to deceive them. They promised the town folk a peace covenant if they surrendered all their arms, and so when the fortieth battle took place, they had no arms and the Turks sorely overpowered them all, but with few killed. Other villages fared not as well. Because there was no communication, all were isolated from one another. Sometimes it would not be until spring, when the snow melted and the passes opened, before they would hear about how an entire village had simply disappeared.

Then the First World War began and the Turks considered this an opportune time to solve, for the last time, the "Armenian Question." While the world powers raged in a life and death struggle, the Turks went on a rampage-type campaign of their own in 1915 with the goal being the extermination and destruction of all Armenians. Not only villages, but towns and cities were ransacked and all ages were either slaughtered or herded into the deserts. Besieged by hunger and thirst, many kinds of diseases, usually typhus, followed them like the shadow of death, most suffering a grueling death.

Hripsime did not learn the true horror of what had happened until she was old enough to bear it and even then she remembered the day well. It was told to her that Muslim Turks, absorbed in a brutal belief system, massacred in the most methodical, most merciless, and worst indescribable ways, over one and half million, to even as many as two million Armenians. Although the Turks justified these actions, the cover up could never explain how most were innocent women, children, and the elderly. Hripsime remembered a pastor saying during an Armenian-American Community Salute at a bicentennial, "Now they can tell the world there is no more 'Armenian Question' because there are no more Armenians."

Hripsime heard over the years that most of the few remaining survivors of this holocaust or ethnic cleansing or genocide, as some call it now, came out of Turkey bewildered and with a feeling of hopelessness. A large portion settled in Syria and in the Middle East where hospitable Arab countries under French Mandate had opened their borders. Still others migrated to Europe and to America.

Little Hripsime, by the merciful providence of God, came under the protection of a boarding school governed by some American missionaries at Marash, a large city in Central Turkey.

She learned later her father had brought her there just before her family had disappeared.

Remembering the loneliness she felt for many years, even after she knew the truth of her abandonment, Hripsime often recalled a particular verse that became her own personal vindication from this ever-present hurt. And, when she realized that God the Father was her father, this too was a special comfort. She now whispered it as if someone were there beside her.

When my father and my mother forsake me, then
the Lord will take me up. (Psalm 27:10)

Tears overcame her words as she thought about this early catastrophic time in her life. Deep remorse filled her, as she thought about the cruelty her parents and relatives must have endured. Always guilt resided within her soul, and as time went along, the greatest puzzlement uppermost in her mind, was why had she survived when almost everyone else had been condemned?

As Hripsime grew into a young woman and later, when she became a Christian, she came to realize that the Christian Armenians that had survived the mass exodus, especially those that had suffered and prevailed, became very strong in their belief that no foreign oppression, persecution or massacre would ever be able to change their faith, their destiny and the love they had for their nation. Still, a few denounced their faith. Some of the young girls even killed themselves rather than to be taken captive. Some changed their names to a Moslem or Turkish name to survive; however, most held fast to the Armenian Christian credence. What kept the Armenian Nation most adhesive was that their nation was the first to adopt Christianity as their state religion, which was determined to be as early as 301 A.D. However, many believed this was why they had come under such repression and near extinction.

This caused Hripsime to often refer to Jesus' words:

> Blessed are ye, when men …persecute you, …for
> my sake. Rejoice, and be exceeding glad: for great
> is your reward in heaven… (Matt 5:11,12)

This underpinning, this confidence that intertwined itself among the Armenians became like a tightly wound ball of string that bound them as one to this heritage. Hripsime felt very much apart of this heritage as well. Still, because of a distinct and unmistakable pattern in her life, because of the many obvious miracles that had kept her alive, she could not help but ask the question, "Why did God want her to survive?"

– Two –

In the distance, Hripsime heard much shooting and then a loud explosion echoed along the row of tall buildings that lined either side of the street. A noise of many people scrambling to safety aroused Hripsime. It penetrated her soul and many thoughts of past wars came alive in her head. Then there was a lull and the streets fell silent once more.

Again, she heard the rush of footsteps outside her door. When they stopped, a sporadic, obtrusive knocking resounded throughout the small fourth-floor flat and the door opened before she could respond.

"You must go to the lower floors for safety," her neighbor shrieked. "They have cut the phone lines! They are here! Can't you hear the shooting? The shelling? Many buildings are crumbling into the streets."

"I will stay here."

"But you must go down below," her anxious neighbor screamed again.

"If a bomb should hit the building, it will crush us even if we are on the lower floor. No. I will stay here. You go though. It is better that you are with the others."

"How is it I need to be with the others and it is all right for you to be alone up here?"

"We will be fine."

"We? Who do you have with you?"

"God, my Heavenly Father, Jesus Christ, my Savior, and the Holy Spirit, my Comforter, plus me makes four," Hripsime said, with a boastful smile.

She praised God silently for this excellent opportunity to witness to the power and the protection of the Holy Trinity, especially in such a difficult situation. During those all too brief moments, she felt that old familiar surge of joy that always came when God brought such opportunities her way, but soon it was gone and the realization of the moment returned when she noticed the fear in her friend's face had not diminished, even a little bit. Her neighbor seemed only able to stand motionless and to stare at Hripsime in disbelief, but then she turned, retreated into the hallway, and shut the door behind her. Hripsime listened to her heavy breathing and heavy footsteps as she ran down the stairs. The whole building was heavy with the tension of those within, but finally all was silent. And soon only distant shoots and an occasional blast that usually brought on the crumbling of a building wall could be heard; Still, all was some distance away.

Hripsime decided to draw on her only recourse for comfort and hope, her Almighty God. She knelt down in prayer beside her kitchen table and prayed for her neighbors and friends, especially for her very frightened neighbor.

In the beginning, during a few of the raids, they huddled together on the lower floors. Eventually they all returned to their own flats and rode it out Hripsime's way. All learned quickly there was no real shelter from the horrible bombs, rockets and bullets, no matter what floor they were on. They also knew, as Hripsime knew, there was no real escape, no way out from their flimsy fortress of cracked concrete walls and ceilings.

Silently, she lay in her bed as she listened to the rockets whistling and then roar when they hit their mark. This unyielding racket carried throughout the entire night. Closer and closer these noises of death approached her tiny cell, one after another, each stronger and louder than the one before. This clamor tried to blast her thoughts from any constructive pattern. The horror of it would have consumed her if she had dwelt on it long enough, but instead, she pictured Jesus sitting at the foot of her bed. His unshakable countenance kept reassuring her. Her thoughts would slip back and forth from His image to a few words of prayer, and then back again to Him. She could not fathom how others got through such a thing without having this comfort— the Lord's comfort.

The next day it was the same. Even the strongest buildings made of cement and bricks shook. She did not know what kept them standing and then eventually one would be a solid hit and it would come crashing down. Along with it would be every piece of furniture and sometimes some poor soul who dwelt within its walls. Sometimes when they came crumbling into the streets below, people would be caught off guard and be standing beneath the collapsing walls. Either bricks or mortar crushed them or shards of glass viciously flew at them slicing them to pieces. Above all, the screams for help were the most unbearable.

Each night seemed worse than the last. In the darkness, Hripsime would lie quietly in her bed. With eyes wide open, her lips would be in constant motion with words that came from deep inside of her. As she listened to the shelling increase and more and more bombs explode, each seemingly stronger and louder than the previous bombardment, she sang praises to God, as if He was her own and nobody else could lay claim to Him. Then the shelling and blasting subsided and she heard only the sound of bullets whistling through the air and pinging against some object, inanimate or animate. Usually, there was a crying out if it was a fleshly penetration. She would pause no matter what she was thinking or doing and pray aloud for that person. The acrid smoke and the stench of death invaded her nostrils, her eyes, her whole body. It had even impregnated her soul. Her dry mouth and swollen throat made it hard to swallow. Much smoke and dust tried to choke away any breathable air. Every now and again, she would wipe away a tear.

Only a dead person could keep from crying in the midst of something like this, she thought almost aloud.

As the hours passed and then the days, there was seemingly no relief. Water especially was a problem. All she had was the little she had wisely saved for drinking. Food came into short supply and, of course, there was no baker of bread. With no electricity and still no way to contact her loved ones, she felt so alone. The others in the building had ferreted themselves inside their flats, as field mice might do when afraid of their predators. Once in awhile she would meet someone in the hallway, but, overall, she was alone, but alone with Jesus at her side.

Once in awhile she would venture out onto her small balcony and peek out at the burning rubble and the empty shells of burning cars that filled the streets. Besides rubble, all streets were full of garbage. The collectors dared not collect it; they feared bombs might be hidden under it.

Those shot and killed in the streets lay where they had fallen. No one dared to pick them up and take them to the cemetery to bury them for there was great fear of a stray bullet or maybe a shell fragment might hit them as they went about their task. Even if it was a loved one, the fear was too strong.

What an unbearable situation it all is, she cried within herself.

Then she heard a commotion in the street and boldly she ventured to her balcony to look out at what was happening. What she saw shocked her. Someone had tied a corpse to the back of a car and it was now dragging the bouncing, flying body behind it. Stoically numb, she could not stop watching the scene until the car disappeared from sight.

Hripsime's feelings almost came out as words, as she thought, *They were just trying to go as far as they could with it, hoping beyond hope to throw the body under a bridge or to take it to some solitary spot. It's just an effort to keep the stink away and to keep the animals from eating the body.*

It was the smell, that stinging, pungent odor of rotting bodies that never could be forgotten. She always feared that these things would never depart from her mind and as the years went along, she found this to be true.

Eventually a proclaimed cease-fire came, but this only made Hripsime and the others in the building more afraid for this could only mean they were preparing to attack with more severity. However, the breather was welcome and again the silence helped her to relax a little.

She now plunged again into her past, as she desperately tried to escape from the horrors that wanted to close in on her from all sides. Then she began to recall her days at the college, the Central Turkey Girl's College, and how again God had miraculously delivered her from death and what should have been.

Although World War I had ended, peace did not come to Turkey. As peace talks dragged on at the Paris Peace Conference in Versailles during 1919 and at other peace tables, wherein Turkey was the main focal point, war still raged on in Turkey until 1923. Not long after the Great War, a large Greek Army with the help of the British and the French invaded Turkey. However, when great Greek massacres took place, the British and French eventually withdrew their support. This brought about a grand revolt wherein a Turkish nationalist movement rose up and enveloped the sad situation. This revolt became known as the Turkish War of Independence.

When the Treaty of Sevres was signed August 10, 1920, this supposedly ended the Ottoman Empire and limited Turkey to the City of Constantinople (Istanbul), to the surrounding territory, and to that part of Asia Minor known as the Anatolia. Although Mohammed VI, the Sultan of Turkey accepted this, it was not acknowledged by the Nationalist leader Mustafa Kemal and he proceeded to successfully overthrow the government and establish the Republic of Turkey in 1923 with Angora (Ankara) as its capital instead of Istanbul.

When the French marched into Marash in 1920, one of the cities where many Armenians had fled during WWI, the intention was to try to gain some control over the matter; however, much rebel resistance awaited them. Sorrowfully, they learned that under the guise of Turkish independence, the leader of this revolt was carrying on with the old Ottoman tradition of exterminating Christian Armenians. This caused Marash to become a bloody hellhole, or the massacre of massacres.

In the afternoon, on one particular day, the warmth from the sun provided exceptional comfort to Hripsime. The day was lovely, inspiring. She had become completely distracted from the disturbing thoughts of the impending war. The birds were singing in the tops of the trees, the brooks were running in the midst of the gardens, and the tiny flowers were peeping out of the ground. The smell in the air was the distinct aroma of spring.

Again, she did not remember her age, but definitely she was in her late teens. Standing in the doorway of one of the main buildings on campus, she covered herself with a large shawl from the top of her head to her feet. This was the custom for a girl to cover her whole body with a shawl or the Turk boys would throw stones at them. When Hripsime stepped out of the campus gate and started for the main part of town, usually a fifty-minute walk, she saw an Armenian soldier coming from the opposite direction.

As he came towards her, he asked, "Where are you going?"

"I am going to the dentist," she said, puzzled at why he was questioning her.

All at once, he grabbed her arm and pushed her back toward the gate. In shock, Hripsime could not speak.

"Hurry, run, get inside and lock the door! The fighting is going to start immediately!"

Just as Hripsime unlatched the gate, the shooting began. Bullets came from every direction, from machine guns, Tommy guns and even cannons. She crouched as she ran for the door of the nearest building. She covered her head with her shawl, as if it might protect her from the bullets. Reaching for the handle of the door, a bullet whisked by her and hit the door just above her head. Quickly, she pushed on the heavy door, rushed inside, and slammed it behind her. She heard more bullets hit the door as she sank to the floor. Rolling away from it, she crawled to a safe corner. Tears streamed down her cheeks as she tried to gather herself. She paused for several minutes in a crouched position in the corner trying to understand what had almost happened to her. If she would have been only a few steps farther from the gate, she would have been shot and killed on the spot!

This is a miracle. Sending a soldier, just at the right time, who kept me from going any farther? Thank you, God, she whispered within herself.

After the fighting was over, a great crowd of Armenians, young, old, middle-aged and teenagers the same as she, went to meet the French Army as they marched through the city. It was a grand demonstration of singing, dancing and shouting with much gratitude for they had come to Marash on behalf of the

Armenians, to fight and deliver them from the Turks. Hripsime ran up to one of the French soldiers who was marching in the ranks and marched along with him. She had picked some fresh flowers from one of the gardens on campus and she now handed them to him.

"Thank you so very much that you are here," she said.

The soldier tipped his hat and with a smile, he accepted the flowers. However, his attention again was on his marching and he looked away as he adjusted his gear and marched on with his unit with little hesitation. Still, Hripsime felt better for doing this and she smiled as she waved at the soldier who only slightly turned again to acknowledge the attention she had given him.

Hripsime's heart sang with joy. The hope that was flowing through her veins gave her great expectations for the future, as she watched the many soldiers gallantly marching through the streets. Later, a rumor broke out and flashed through the city like a bolt of lightening. Because the Turks had seen the Armenians massing around the soldiers and had heard their shouts of joy, this had filled them with a furious anger. They now became even more anxious and more determined to take their revenge out on the Armenians.

The college campus comprised of several large and small buildings housing sixty students and teachers. Built at the foot of a high mountain, the bulk of the French armies stationed themselves there. Digging in, surrounding the campus, from this high position, they could defend the entire city. However, this meant the Turks directed their main attack at the school.

With a vengeance, with such a flurry of bombs and bullets, they almost annihilated them all. The barracked brave French soldiers shot round after round into the many hoards of Turks, who came at them one wave after another.

All the windows on the fourth floor of the main building, where the dorm was located, were either cracked from bullets or completely shot out. Most of the time, this was where Hripsime and the others watched the fighting; however, it was hard to look upon one atrocity after another. At one point, it became so dangerous it was necessary to scurry to the lower regions. The library, which was on the second floor, was used the most. During a lull, they all ran back upstairs to gather some blankets and pillows. When they returned, each found their own safe corner in which to sit or sleep. Some bunched together for the warmth and the security of one body next to the other. Hripsime sat alone in one particular corner, her corner. The dining room on the first floor was another safe place for they had covered the windows with sandbags, but as Hripsime thought about it, there really was no safe haven.

The bullets and shelling were unspeakably terrifying. Fires erupted in some parts of the building. Luckily, the French soldiers came from their trenches and helped douse them. This spared most of the buildings, but some rooms were so charred, they were inhabitable. When the fighting became too intense, the students and teachers hovered into small clusters. Shivering with fear, they held onto one another waiting for their end

Oh, how hopeless it all seemed, she thought.

In the trenches, one particular bloody onslaught killed so many on both sides that there was a ceasefire just to clear away the dead and the wounded; otherwise, the piles of rotting corpses would have hampered the fighting. Even the horses did not escape the many heavy attacks. When a horse was shot, in order to feed the army, the French would butcher it and cook it in huge vats in the laundry room.

In another large building of equal size, which was on the other side of a road from the building where Hripsime and the other students were hiding, was a building the army used as a hospital for the wounded. After the initial blitz and when there was any kind of a pause in the fighting, Hripsime and some of her school friends would venture across the road and visit the many wounded to try to cheer them. They were handsome young men, lying in hopeless conditions. Many were missing legs and arms. Hripsime wanted to do more, but did not know what to do. Whenever she returned from the hospital, her spirit would be crushed with despair; the suffering was so great. Still, she was one of the first to go the next time there was a chance. She often thought that this was where her desire came from to be a nurse later in her life.

The fighting went on for a long time. Many houses and buildings within the city burned and became rubble, but the school still stood even though it took one beating after another. The death toll was massive; both sides suffered enormous casualties. Many civilians died as well, usually when someone ran to find a safer corner.

At one point, the French almost defeated the Turks and they retreated into the mountains that surrounded Marash. They hid themselves in the caves of the rocks, but after awhile they snuck down into the town again. Sporadically, they would attack in small bands. This made it impossible to go downtown to purchase food, that is, if there was any. Some of the students with the help of the matron of the boarding school attempted to make their own bread by baking it over a wood fire in the yard. Ready-made canned food had disappeared at the beginning of the conflict, and then eventually they ran out of all foodstuffs. Because there were no facilities of any kind such as stoves or iceboxes, most went hungry. If there was something to eat, they ate it; if not, they learned to go without.

One unforgettable day, while Hripsime was crossing from one building to another, a bullet came screeching through the air and brushed her hair. When it whistled by, it passed very close to her ear. Startled, she could not move for several seconds. She imagined if it had been one inch closer, it might have blown her brain from her skull, just as she had seen happen to one of the soldiers she had accidentally come upon one day.

This was yet another miracle, she thought.

After a few weeks past, they then heard the most shocking news of all. The French Army announced they were withdrawing. This news spread through the town and the school like wildfire. Everyone knew instantly what this meant. There would be a horrible massacre of the entire Armenian community. All the inhabitants of Marash knew the Turks were hanging on for such an opportunity.

Hripsime now recalled Miss Blakely, the President of their college, an American, a grand person and good president. All the students admired and respected her, although they did think she was a strict disciplinarian. One look from the top of her eyeglasses was sufficient to know she was not pleased with something they might have done. Hripsime knew Miss Blakely favored her as was one of her dearest students, as Hripsime often read to her from the Turkish newspapers.

At seven o'clock that evening, shortly after the horrible news of the French Army's withdrawal, Miss Blakely came down to the dining room where everyone had assembled with much fear. The room was abuzz as all were waiting with great expectation as to what she would tell them they should do next. Everyone knew this was a very difficult situation and when she entered, all were in quiet anticipation. The tension was so heavy, it seemed as if someone were sucking the air from her lungs. Barely able to breath, Hripsime waited for what seemed an eternity. Nervously, Miss Blakely paced and rang her hands together as she tried to talk. Finally, she spoke a few words.

"If the Turks attack our campus and take away all of you girls, I have no power or any means to protect you," she said, as she looked over at Hripsime with tears in her eyes.

Hripsime and her friends looked at one another with great shock on their faces as they listened to Miss Blakely's unbelievable words. For some time, she stood unresponsive as did each of her friends. No one said anything. The quiet was deafening.

Then, as if Miss Blakely could not talk anymore, because her emotional state was very high, she simply turned and solemnly left the room. This had been an all too brief recitation in Hripsime's mind. Then each student, including Hripsime, slowly retreated and huddled in their respective corners or under a table with their blankets and pillows in tow. Hripsime's imagination now ran rampant with what might happen next and she could only think of the darkest and the most hideous.

In the meantime, a severe snowstorm had began. As Hripsime took her coat sleeve and wiped away the frost from one of the windows, she noticed, as she looked out into the night, the snowflakes swirled about furiously before they touched the ground and that there was already a great accumulation. Then she ran to the door and opened it to peer out, but the storm overwhelmed her and the wind blew with such force, it was impossible to hold on to the door. As she called out to the others for help in closing it, she could see the storm was indeed too intense to be out in it.

"We must escape with the French army. We will surely die if we stay here," Hripsime said to one of her friends.

"I hear dying in a snowstorm is not all that bad. It couldn't be as painful as a bullet or a blow from the blade of a sword. I hear you just get real sleepy and then you go to sleep and never wake up," another classmate shared.

"Even if we freeze and die, it is much better to die in the snowstorm than to go through whatever the Turks have in mind for us."

Several others were nearby and heard the conversation and soon there were twelve of them who had decided to escape by following the French Army.

One girl cried out, "It will take a long time in the storm to reach the railroad station and to catch up with the army. We will have to walk. There is no transportation of any kind. All the horses are dead."

"We must try," Hripsime said.

Desperately she tried to squelch the hysteria that was mounting inside of her. She must be more convincing in getting them to see it her way.

"We will have to walk through the deep snow and we wouldn't be able to see even a few steps in front of us," another negative voice bellowed.

"We must do something," Hripsime again responded.

Finally, the twelve decided to go along with Hripsime, that this was their only hope, so they started to devise a plan. Hripsime, seemingly the ring leader of the small band of believers, remembered how very alone she and her friends had felt in their life and death struggle, as the others jeered and scorned such an undertaking. However, the daring dozen forged ahead with all kinds of preparations for their departure. They put on as many layers of clothing as possible: several layers of stockings, one on top of the other, mittens, scarves, and much more. The matron of the boarding house even opened the store and gave them some dry food, which they packed into pillowcases that they used as bags. Standing in front of the heavy door, ready to do what they felt they had to do, they all stood with downcast expressions on their faces. All knew deep down the hopelessness of their situation. As they wept, cried and hugged one another, they called to God to help them.

All of a sudden, Miss Hardy, the American piano teacher, appeared. Hearing their noise, she came running into the entry room. Seeing their distress, she put her arms around them like a mother and said, "My dear girls, what is all this commotion? What is the matter?"

"We are planning to escape with the French Army, to die in the snowstorm most likely," Hripsime said, with tears streaming down her cheeks.

"I will never let you escape with the army. If I die, you also will die with me. If not, we will live together here under the protecting arms of our Heavenly Father."

Therefore they gave up the idea of escaping in this way. In Hripsime's mind, God had sent Miss Hardy just at the right time to stop them from their sad plight. This sad and uncertain plight had been almost more than Hripsime had been able to bear. A terrible confusion had reigned inside of her, as it was a certain death situation, but still before it had seemed so clear to her that it was better than waiting for death to come to them.

This she felt had been another miracle, as the enemy never came to kill them or take them away by force. Hripsime now thumbed through her mind as if thumbing through the pages of the Bible until one particular verse in the Psalms stuck in her thoughts:

...And, call upon me in the day of trouble: I will deliver thee, and thou shalt glorify me. (Psalm 50:15)

After the French Army left, many families gathered and took refuge in the churches and school buildings in the town. And, when the Turks came out of hiding from the mountains and converged upon the town, they burned all the churches and school buildings. Mercilessly, they scaled the walls and poured kerosene onto the roofs. Hripsime and her classmates stood dumbfounded as they watched on high from the fourth floor through broken windows. It seemed like the flames and smoke of the fires reached the heavens.

The helplessness she felt at that moment caused her to double to her knees. Crouching down below the windowsill, she found she could not bear to look upon the grueling scene anymore. Hripsime trembled with fear as she tried to shut out the awful screams and cries for help that came from the burning buildings, but nothing took away this penetrating uproar. It flooded her every thought and the horror kept on and on in her mind. When she learned one of their teachers was among the ill-fated, she could not stop the words that spilled from inside her aching heart.

"Oh God, have mercy on us all," she said, as she still languished below the window, watching the glare of the fires on the opposite wall.

That day became a day of mourning and weeping for them all and for all Armenians everywhere for many years afterward. Hundreds of thousands of children of all ages along with babes in the arms of their mothers died on that unforgettable, horrible day. The Turks had finally finished their revenge of many long years.

There were a few who had escaped by following the French Army that snowy night, but no one really knew if they had gotten away for sure, as they were never heard from again. And, so it was concluded that most perished that dreadful day and night. Only the students and teachers at the school miraculously survived.

As she thought back over the years and the many times she would awake screaming in a cold sweat, Hripsime thought aloud, "Surely, this was yet another miracle that only could have come from God. But why did just a handful survive and why was she among the very few?"

The question of why she had survived already followed her since she had heard about the loss of her parents and family, now this would intensify and hound her through out the whole of her life. As never before it followed her like a shadow at its deepest and strongest moment.

– Three –

The concussion from a bomb that exploded nearby sent sound waves through the air that rocked Hripsime's bed and caused her ear drums to feel as if they might explode. Her head throbbed, as it did after every blast, but this explosion was stronger and louder than any had been before. This night seemed extra long and Hripsime's eyes never closed. Sometimes all she thought of was how much she wanted to shut her eyes and how much she wanted to sleep. The fatigue and tiredness she felt every minute of each day during these times sometimes consumed all thought. The walls of her tiny fourth-floor flat shuddered and wobbled relentlessly. The light fixture over the kitchen table swung like a pendulum nonstop. The target of late seemed to be only the Christian Quarter.

On one of the worst days, when there were many explosions on every side of her building, she became so frightened she latched onto her Bible from the nightstand and ran to the corner behind the bedroom door. She sat on the floor reading for how long she was not sure, but the comfort of His encouraging promises was all that mattered to her, as she knew that this was the only thing that could squelch the terror inside of her.

Then praying aloud, reaching to the heavens, she said, "Lord, if it's for me to stay here and be killed with the many others who are being killed daily, let Thy will be done, but if it is your will, Lord, open a way for me and my loved ones to escape from this awful fighting. Thy will be done."

Whenever there was a lull or a cease-fire, she would timidly venture out onto her balcony where she could watch the commotion below her. Everybody, parents and children, and older people were running into the streets to try to find out if someone was selling some vegetables, fruits or any kind of food, but fresh was the most desirous. Fortunately, sometimes during a night when there was a lull, some of the young, brave men would go to their villages in the mountains and to their gardens to gather whatever was leftover from the enemy. Then they would bring it to the city and spread it on a piece of cloth on one of the street corners and sell it to gain some money, risking their lives as they did this. Several times Hripsime would venture out into the calamity of the streets to buy from them.

On one particular day, she saw that attention was being made to one corner about two blocks away. Quite a crowd was gathering. Hripsime ran back into the kitchen, grabbed a tote bag, and headed down the four flights of stairs at a fast pace. Then after a moment of caution and a moment of prayer, she flew into the street and headed for the crowd. She noted to herself how everything one did these days was with the utmost haste that there was never a moment when she was not strung tighter than a freshly tuned piano wire. Only those times when she was reading the Word of God was there any peace.

When she reached the aggregate of yelling, high-pitched voices and arms that flailed about with tightly clutched fists of money, she tried to worm her way to the front to see if anything was left. All were shoving and pushing and at the height of the buying and selling frenzy, Hripsime found herself helplessly squashed between two very large women. Finally, she was able to look into the face of one of the men she recognized from other times she had bought food, and he recognized her. Beckoning to her to come his way, somehow she cut through the craziness. After bargaining for a few things, she made her purchase and made her way through the crowd again. Then, all at once, the crowd stood erect as one and they all listened. Bullets were whistling through the air. A few still kept on with their frantic exchange, but most reacted with much panic. In the midst of the tumult, somehow Hripsime was able to break away and run with her small bundle of precious food. And then a nearby blast curdled the airwaves and everyone scattered in different directions; all wanted to find a safe corner somewhere. Hripsime instinctively ran the direction of her building, but it was two blocks away. When she reached a doorway, she ducked into it and paused. Looking back at the scene she had just left, horror struck her dumb at what she saw. Some found safety as she had, but many had been shot and were either dead or dying. The dying were moaning or screaming for help. She knew if anyone ventured toward them to help, a bullet or shell fragment would find them too, so she stood there and waited helpless. Trying to hold in all the terrible turmoil inside of her, she prayed.

A man was running toward her; however, as she reached out to him, he fell to the ground with a thud only a few feet away. A pool of blood circled his head and grew larger as she watched. As she mulled over in her mind his motionless body, Hripsime knew he was dead.

Not able to restrain herself any longer, she crouched and started to run. Scabby, puss filled, bloody bodies pocked the street like a poorly designed carpet. Dodging many bullets, she worked her way through the bodies and the rubble. Even in her hurried state, as she approached each body, she would stop to see if they were recognizable and if they were truly dead; there might be something she could do. It seemed like she was in slow motion and for sure, a bullet would soon find her just like it had found these poor souls beneath her feet. Treacherously slow, her progress was at a snail's pace. However, at last she reached her building and when she ducked inside the doorway, a big sigh of relief came from deep within her. She stood there leaning against the wall panting for several seconds until she caught her breath. And, too, she needed to clear her mind from the panic that wanted to chase her mind around. As she climbed the dark stairway, she listened to the chaos outside and was thankful God had spared her life, as it was clear most did not make it from that frenzied circle of buyers.

The stairs seemed very laborious no matter how slowly she maneuvered her way up them. Piles of debris from the walls and the ceilings made the path upwards like an obstacle course. She had not remembered so much clutter when she had gone down them a short time before and deduced a bomb must have fallen too close. She then wondered if her flat had been spared. With no electricity or the light it provided, the way up was never easy, but this time the stairway seemed extra hard to climb.

Maybe it's my frenzied state of mind, she thought

Once on her floor, she could not unlock the door fast enough. Desperately, she fumbled with the key as the heavy tote bag swung back and forth under her arm. Once the door was open, she flew inside. Slamming it shut, she locked the door and lay against it trying to catch her breath once again. She chuckled more from hysteria than anything.

Did she really think she was safe from all the bullets and bombs behind this locked door?

Eventually, she walked toward the kitchen table and set her precious bundle on the white linen tablecloth that had pieces of plaster upon it. Slumping down into one of the straight back chairs, limp from exhaustion, she felt exasperated beyond anything she had ever felt before. Her heart would not stop pounding. It beat so hard it seemed as if it might come out of her chest. She could not believe what had just happened. Quickly she decided that only the most desperate situation would drive her into the streets again.

That night, as it was every night, even the lighting of a small candle was dangerous, as it could be seen from great distances. As soon as the enemy saw any light, they would attack in that direction. So Hripsime determined that having no electricity was a blessing, if for no other reason. Therefore, she decided to dine the next day and put away her invaluable eatables; she was to distraught to eat anyway. While she lay in her bed in the dark, it seemed as if her emotions might take control of her. Always, every minute was a struggle between life and death, but at night, these thoughts seem to close in on her more than during the day. The fear, horror and the emotions felt by all during these times was too hard to bear and so to shut it out of their minds, most tried to pretend they were somewhere else, as she now began to do once again.

Then Hripsime thought of those things that pertain to God and her mind began to calm itself. She started thinking about the many who were sincere believers in Beirut who cried to God to help them in some way or another, but mostly to spare their lives and lessen the pain during these terrible times. As she thought about this, Hripsime began to believe God was sparing many lives because they were believers and she began to feel more confidence about how he would spare her as well.

Then Hripsime's thoughts turned to the unsaved. These times were full of opportunities for her and other true believers to tell others of the precious promises of God in the Bible; those who never had read or paid any attention to the Word of God before were now open to the truth more than ever before.

One verse that kept coming to her mind was a verse when God was asked by Abraham:

...For ten righteous men? And God said he would

not destroy the city for ten's sake. (Genesis 18:32)

And, so Hripsime began to pray as she had never prayed before, not for herself, but for those around her and then she remembered another verse where God said to Isaiah:

The Lord saw that there was no man, and wondered

why there was no intercessor. (Isaiah 59:16)

Then her prayers turned to intercessory prayer, not only for those she loved, her family, her neighbors and friends, but for the entire Christian Quarter, for Beirut, for Lebanon, for the leaders, and for all those in authority. She asked God for a once again tranquil and quiet life for the Lebanese.

"Oh, Father, if it could only be as it was before," she whispered.

Before long Hripsime fell asleep and she slept hard for the first time in many days with dreams of how her Beirut was before. Beirut had been a cosmopolitan city. The culture, a mixture of East and West, European and Arab, had attracted over a million and half people to its shores by 1975. Many considered it the Paris of the Middle East. A famous port, it was a banking and cultural center for this region of the world. This narrow coastal plain contained by the massive Lebanon Mountains that steeply rose to the east, created an exceptional Mediterranean climate of warm, dry summers and cool, wet winters. The only hampering element was the spatial distribution between the major ethnic and religious groups: the different sects of Muslims and the Christians and Jews. A fundamental division, an unofficial line that ran between two hills, divided the city. This valley was where Beirut was originally founded, but now it divided the ethnic and religious cultures of the city. The Lebanese Shiite Muslims inhabited Musaytibah, West Beirut and the Lebanese Sunni Muslims and Lebanese Christians inhabited Ashrafiyah, East Beirut, each with their own sector. The tourists flocked to the high-rises and hotels along the shoreline on the Avenue de Paris.

After the 1967 Israeli War, in the late 1960s and early 1970s, an increasing number of Palestinian Muslims began to pour into West Beirut and expanded the city southward. Coming with these refugees was a new movement, the PLO (The Palestine Liberation Organization). Led by Yasser Arafat, he passionately sought out a homeland for his people and Lebanon became their primary objective during this time. Uprooted in 1948, when Israel was proclaimed a state in order to accommodate the 750,000 Jewish refugees who came out of WWII, cohabitation never became a solution for the Palestinians and Israelis. Henceforth, an uproar ensued from this time forward, without any end in sight.

The PLO, begun in 1964, derived from a group known as the Fatah, thrived in Jordan until King Hussein kicked them out. After 1967, when the Arab nations cut loose from Arafat and his cause, he began to push his Palestinians in a new direction. For the next 10 years, their goal was a massive terrorist campaign with their main objective the destruction of Israel. After Arafat and the PLO fled from Jordan to Syria and then settled in Southern Lebanon, this affected Beirut greatly. As they became a stronger established community in the early seventies, this caused much political deterioration and an immense upheaval in Beirut. In 1972 the PLO reached a high point when PLO raiders murdered eleven athletes at the Munich Olympics. This brought much condemnation upon them, but to no avail. In 1973, they murdered a US Ambassador and others in Sudan, but with no retaliation. In October, 1973 they became recognized by the UN and in November, 1974 the PLO became the sole legitimate representation of the Palestinian people.

When Hripsime and her family first moved to Beirut from Aleppo around 1956, she thought it was the most beautiful city in the world with its universities, hospitals, foreign embassies, museums, and high-rise luxury hotels along the beach. With a mixture of European and Arab influences, this very cosmopolitan city, held many pleasures for Hripsime and her family. From their flat, she would walk to the downtown area and buy anything they needed. The shops and outdoor cafes were splendid in every way. However, when 1967 came and tensions began to rise, any existence was hampered with thoughts of what the future held.

The tension between the PLO and the other Muslims was particularly high; the PLO extremists wanted to bring back the old ways. A shiver went up and down Hripsime's spine and her feet shook in her shoes when she thought of the old ways; this is what had destroyed her family and almost annihilating all Armenians.

In addition to this, every time Israel and the Palestinians had any kind of a skirmish, refugees would flood southern Lebanon and Beirut. Overcrowded and poverty stricken, a shanty-type of existence skirted the city and had become an overwhelming problem, especially for the governing bodies.

Still, the main problem in Beirut was the PLO and how they tried to push their ways upon the masses. As they took a stronger hold on the Moslem population, a large rift grew between the Muslims and soon there were three major factions all warring against one another: the PLO and its sympathizers, the anti-PLO Muslims that included the Shiite and Sunni sects and their divergences, and the Christians. By 1975, Hripsime and the rest of the Christian Quarter were feeling the full effects of what would be one of the most vicious civil wars ever recorded, one that would seemingly find no end.

When the shooting stopped, usually everyone would come out of their corner and go out onto their balcony, if they had one. On one such occasion, when Hripsime was standing on her tiny platform, she heard the terrible clamor of a windowpane shattering. She stood silently on her balcony, very frightened, trying to locate the origin of the breaking glass. To her great surprise, it was her landlord's balcony directly below her that had been hit. If the rocket or whatever it was had come two meters higher, it would have killed her.

Then the words spilt from her mouth before she knew what she was saying, "Praise God."

Again, another close call, another miracle, Hripsime thought, but then she prayed for her landlord and his family.

Once, as Hripsime looked out, the viewpoint from her small balcony took another twist. She noticed all four sides of her building had considerable damage and this reminded her again of Marash. When she retreated back into her flat and back to her usual safe corner, she returned to her memories when she was a young teen at the girl's college and again she began to recall the terrible French and Turkish conflict in Marash.

After the Turks had decimated the city and all of its occupants, some of the remaining survivors from the town came to the college, as these were the only buildings left standing. Although the situation was strained, Hripsime and a few of her surviving classmates continued their classes until the Americans made preparations to move out of Marash and out of Turkey as it was not safe for anyone anymore, especially an Armenian like herself.

Many of the Armenians of Marash had special talents. Many loved music and had good voices and many of the girls had come to the college to take music lessons. Hripsime too had wanted to learn to play the piano, but never asked about it as she could not afford it. She was an orphan without money and thought such a thing was impossible.

One day after school, she was trying to play and sing a familiar hymn in one of the music rooms, when the music teacher, Miss Hardy, appeared in the doorway. This teacher was the one who had kept them from escaping with the French Army.

"I wondered who was singing and playing the piano so beautifully," Miss Hardy exclaimed.

Hripsime startled, could only look her way, while she stopped what she was doing.

"Would you like to take music lessons, Hripsime?" Miss Hardy asked.

"Yes, very much, but I have no means to pay for this."

After several days, Miss Hardy returned with a plan and said, "I promise to give you lessons on the condition that you take on the responsibility of maintaining and caring for the whole music building."

Hripsime thought for only a few seconds and said gleefully, "Yes, of course."

Now the music building was a huge building in the middle of an orchard on the campus. It had three stories! On the second floor there was a piano and an organ in each room. A grand piano in a very big hall took up the top floor. This was where they had special musical gatherings on special and happy occasions. The bottom floor was like a basement. As she thought about Miss Hardy's proposal, she realized this was a very heavy responsibility, but she had promised and so she took care of the big building: cleaning, dusting, locking the rooms after school and then opening them before classes in the morning. Loaded with her other work, it was still a joy to her for she dearly wanted to learn to play the piano. Therefore, soon after she started these chores, Miss Hardy began giving her lessons. She progressed daily, but it only lasted a few months. It was a sad thing that it all ended, but plans were set in motion for them all to move away from Marash and the college closed its doors for good.

Any Armenians that had survived began to migrate to Syria or elsewhere, but most crossed just the one border to Syria that was open to them under a French mandate. And, so Hripsime, her classmates and some of the American teachers embarked on a treacherous journey with their objective as Aleppo, Syria. The terrain was not easy for horse-drawn wagons full of whatever they could take with them, mostly the most precious. Much was simply left behind. Up to the top of one ridge, down into a vale and then up again onto a plateau-type pasture was the sequence of their arduous journey. This rolling, grassy, treeless, steppe-like terrain, called the plain of Al Jazirah, caused their travel to be a back and forth and up and down pattern that took much longer than if there had been a road with some straightness to it. Usually the caravan of lost souls went along the tops of the ridges and in single file as if it were a funeral procession. Some formations stripped in earth-like colors girded the region, but as a whole a dull gray dominated the landscape. Hripsime found herself often looking back at the dark slate-like mountains of Turkey. Although they provided a magnificent backdrop, this saddened Hripsime because they were becoming more and more distant. Except for the rivers, this region was morbidly barren, without life.

When they reached the large Euphrates River, Hripsime was taken back by the sharp contrast of the scenery along the river. A wonder to look at, Hripsime's eyes rested on a fresh blue ribbon that dramatically rippled between two full stripes of green. Gray, rocky, desolate cliffs bordered the blue-green belt that went on without end. The dreariness and the colornessless of the cliffs and buttes caused the river and its surroundings to come even more alive. The green vegetation was of a limited variety, but still a welcome sight. Still, a fear started to grow in her now as the mountains and its particular kind of vegetation gradually disappeared from sight and the flatness and blandness increased around her. She had never been away from her mountains before.

Another sadness that produced itself was the dreadful recollection that this might have been the very same path taken by her parents and family in the 1915 deportation. This horrid remembrance did not leave her alone for some time no matter how she tried to detour her thinking.

Slowly, but surely the small caravan of scholars and teachers and students finally caught sight of Aleppo, as it crept onto the horizon. Located in the northern part of Syria, Aleppo (Halab) was midway between the Mediterranean Sea and the Euphrates River. Hripsime had never seen anything like it before; she had never seen a major metropolis. The ancient city, one of the oldest cities, second to Damascus, rested on a plateau, 1,400 feet high.

In the beginning, Hripsime found much distress in her new surroundings. The few trees and the sparse vegetation was a normal expectancy for what Aleppo should look like; however, this barrenness in comparison to the evergreens and undergrowth around Marash was a harsh reminder of what she had left behind. She also missed the snow, but gradually she became accustomed to the radically different climate. Syria was very different from the mountainous terrain of Marash. The summers were hot and dry and the winters were wet and mild.

Also, Aleppo's size was a calamitous change as well. It was well over a million people, but these were people who lived without fear and this was a big plus in Hripsime's mind. Because of its size, there was much to do and to see. A city of history, it consisted of an old and a new town; the former was enclosed by a wall dating from medieval times. Settled by the Hittites before 1000BC, in the Third Century AD, it became the greatest center of trade between Europe and lands farther east. However, when the Suez Canal was built, this diminished Aleppo's importance. Hripsime found this history to be of great interest; it gave the city much diversity and character.

After the initial adjustment, she found much excitement in this newfound world and she could not wait to explore it to the fullest. As time went by, a rail connected the city with Beirut and Damascus and it became a dream of Hripsime's that some day she would visit these cities as well. She also was very thankful she was in good company; this helped her to adjust and kept her from a feeling of being totally alone.

Some items packed away in the wagons brought from Marash were textbooks and the already printed diplomas for Hripsime and six of her classmates. Although they had completed their courses at the Central Turkey Girl's College, they had to leave before they were properly presented. And, so it happened, these seven received their diplomas and graduated from the college. Hripsime could not thank God enough for she felt He had given her a unique opportunity not only in bringing her to this college, but in allowing her to continue her education in such hard circumstances. Unlike the other students who had paid, she had worked hard by doing all kinds of extra work during her free hours. Always she had felt her education was a special blessing from God. She knew that even at a young age this would eventually give her a tremendous advantage down the road, much more than if she had been an illiterate, as it was with most of the orphans. And, as it turned out this was of extreme importance when the time came for her to marry.

A few years before the school closed, one of Hripsime's Armenian college teachers had gone to America to join her sister and two brothers, who had migrated there a few years before. When this teacher from the past learned that the college was going to close, she contacted the President, Miss Blakely, about Hripsime and wrote that she wanted her to send Hripsime to the States at the first opportunity so she could marry her younger brother. After reading the letter, Miss Blakely approached Hripsime and told her about the proposal and tried to persuade her to go this way that this was a grand opportunity for her. The marriage would take place as soon as she reached the States and then all her needs would be fulfilled.

"What more could a young girl like you want more than this," Miss Blakely bluntly relayed.

Even though this teacher was one of Hripsime's favorites, she was afraid of this proposal. She had no idea what kind of young man this teacher's brother was, as she had never heard her talk of him. She now remembered that during the years before this teacher left, Hripsime had been aware she had been watching her very closely, but unaware until now as to why.

In these days, parents, elder sisters or brothers decided who was to marry their sister or brother and since Hripsime was an orphan, she guessed she was fair game to anyone that came along and wanted to find her a mate. If elders saw fit, it was finished and no one resisted usually. The girl or boy could hardly object, for this was the way it was and the common knowledge was that older people were more experienced and more mature than the younger set. Therefore, in this situation, Hripsime felt extremely frustrated and the only way out was to cry to God. She prayed that He would help her solve this problem in such a way that she would not hurt her dear teacher. For her, she felt the answer had to be no by all means, but still she prayed and prayed and prayed.

Although, God was not her intimate God in her thoughts at this time, she still felt she had no other alternative. Her thinking was that surely, this would be what her parents wanted her to do. She did not remember how long she struggled with this problem, but she did remember the weight of it almost crushed her spirit. In the meantime, the teacher and her brother sent her a ring and some gifts while Hripsime just kept praying the same prayer over and over again.

When she arrived in Aleppo with Miss Hardy and the others, she came to live with the family of the youngest brother of the teacher who wanted her to come to the States. This brother had also recently moved to Syria with his wife, two small children and their aged father. They all waited patiently for their papers and visas to come so they could go to the States, that is, all except Hripsime.

After several months, when papers did come, they left for America leaving the old father with Hripsime. For some reason, her papers had not come and he could not go because of his age. So, she stayed with him and took care of him, doing all the cooking, cleaning and washing. Then at last a letter came from the teacher, which explained that American law would not permit her brother to bring his fiancée to the States. He had not become a citizen even after living in the States for more than fifteen years. Hripsime later heard he had chosen not to become a naturalized citizen to avoid serving in the army. She also learned that he was uneducated with not even a high school education. They wrote in the letter how very, very sorry they were, but Hripsime was very, very relieved.

Therefore, she felt God once again answered her prayers in a wonderful, miraculous way. Also, she found out later that God had a different and better plan for her as to whom she should marry.

When the old father heard that the whole matter was hopelessly cancelled, he fell on her neck, kissing her and weeping bitterly. He told Hripsime he loved her very much. She felt hard pressed to leave him, but she found someone else to care for him and moved in with another family she had known at the college in Marash. Dr. Poladian, a distinguished member of the College Board, and his wife had just arrived in Aleppo and they invited her to stay in their home as a boarder. His wife had been one of Hripsime's teachers in Marash, so they knew her and knew she had no one, no relatives, no money…nothing. As time went by, Dr. Poladian offered her a teaching position at the Armenian Evangelical School in Aleppo where she then taught for the next two years.

During the first year as a teacher at the school, one of the other teachers invited her to her house for a dinner. Among other guests, there was a young man whom she had not seen before. Before she knew it, she was in a conversation with him and he was asking, "Have you been born again?"

What a shock it was for her to see all the guests watching her for her answer. Politely, she did not answer, but inwardly she was very angry and frustrated, thinking it was none of his business. Later when she really became a born-again Christian, at age 16, no one could keep her quiet about it, for she was so full of the joy of salvation that she wanted to tell everyone she met on the street.

These days were truly some of the happiest most joyful times of my life, she thought.

Then her mind bounced back to present day and sorrow agitated her spirit again. Bombs were now falling again on all sides of her building. Yes, she was back in Beirut; however, that particular night she fell into a deep slumberous sleep and awoke the next day not remembering the shelling that previous night, although she knew it most assuredly had taken place.

Throughout the whole day, she kept envisioning that special moment when she accepted Jesus into her life. These thoughts seemed to fully sustain her as she shut out the horrors around her. It was as if the Holy Spirit had actually taken her back to that moment of salvation as she floated about her fourth-floor flat. She envisioned two angels and the three of them danced upon the clouds. On either side of her, holding her arms, the trio bounced from one cloud to the next in a triumphant jubilation.

– Four –

The next day, Hripsime's mind quickly popped back and did not stray from the present, as one particular explosion seemed directly under her feet.

This time it has hit our building, she thought.

The building shook with such a tremendous force she was sure it was going to tumble to the ground with her amid the debris. This added new cracks to the already existing ones on the walls; the old seemed insignificant compared to the new. More plaster fell from the ceiling. One large piece knocked her to the floor. White dust coated her hair, her face, her whole body. Breathing became difficult and she now struggled toward the sliding door that would take her to the balcony. When she slid it open, thinking there would be fresh air to breathe, the acrid smell of death and burning corpses filled her nostrils and she found no relief. Still, she ventured out curious as to what was happening in the street. Overcome by the devastation around her, she turned to go inside, but then something caught her attention. Noticing the war-torn building next to her, she began to think about her dear neighbors that lived just opposite her balcony and wondered how they were fairing. They were a lovely young Christian family: a Lebanese husband, his English wife and two-bright eyed, beautiful children, nine and six years old. Because this building was higher than hers, it was more exposed to the dangerous bombardments, and they lived on the sixth floor. Now she realized she had not seen them since the start of the shelling and bullets and wondered if they had escaped from Beirut. For a long moment, she thought about this for herself. Many seemed to be leaving. Maybe this war would never end? Maybe this should be her plight as well? However, God would have to provide the way.

Later that morning there was a longer than usual lull. The quiet was discomforting, but still it was a good opportunity to venture out to see if she could find some food. Making her way down the stairs with her empty tote bag, she finally reached the street. Arduously, she trudged through the rubble holding a hanky over her nose, trying to stifle in vain the stench. Some smashed cars lined one side of the narrow street. Most were still burning, even those that had been shelled several days before.

Then Hripsime found herself walking in the direction of her friend's building next door. Her thoughts were full of the bitter, choking stench of human flesh rotting. All at once, a figure of a man darted from out of nowhere, and before she could stop, they collided. As she gathered herself, she realized that this was the husband of the Christian friends that lived in the taller building.

"Hripsime!" he said, when finally he looked up from his rapt gaze into the maze before him.

"How are the children? Are you planning to leave Beirut?" Hripsime asked, downhearted because they had not left yet.

"We have no where to go. We're making out. We've set up housekeeping in the hallway by the elevator where the bullets can't reach us as easy. There's just enough space for a mattress, but we feel more secure there."

"This sounds very hard for you and the children."

"But it's safer, Hripsime, much safer. A few nights ago, a bullet came in from the window behind the elevator. It hit the opposite wall and ricocheted into the corner where our little girl was sleeping. Hripsime, it tore off the upper and lower parts of her pajamas, but without touching her body," he said, with a tone of amazement.

"Oh! My!" Hripsime cried out astounded.

"Ever since that happened, we just can't praise the Lord enough. My wife hangs on to those pajamas as if they were the shroud of Jesus himself. She says they are a sign of God's protecting power and a testimony to anyone who doesn't seem able to believe in His wonderful miracles."

"Come over for a visit the next time there is some quiet and we will pray and sing praises to God together," Hripsime said, gleefully. Then she felt a smile spread across her face. It seemed strange to her to be smiling, as this was the first time in a long time.

At that moment, a shell whistled through the air and they looked at each other with terror in their eyes. Ducking, they watched it pass over there heads and into a building on the next street. Before they parted, they embraced and Hripsime prayed a short prayer for the little family. A warm feeling rushed through the whole of her body, as she walked along. This brief encounter had produced something she had not experienced for some time—the mixing with other Christian souls. What a grand moment this had been and she carried it with her the rest of that day.

After that the family came over whenever they could and they would all blot out the outside world as they prayed and sang praises to God. The Christian fellowship extraordinarily uplifted them all. Although it was only a temporary fix, it helped them forget for a short time the devastation that was around them and those wearisome thoughts about what might happen next.

On one Sunday morning, when they had just gotten together at Hripsime's, a bomb exploded nearby. The concussion caused plaster to fall and everyone ducked or hid under the kitchen table. After a few minutes, when the floor and walls stopped shaking and the dust finally settled, Hripsime and the husband ran to the balcony to look. More than half of this family's building next door was crumbling to the ground. Screams for help penetrated Hripsime's soul.

After he told his wife to stay with the children, the husband and Hripsime flew down the cumbersome stairs and into the street. As they looked in horror, they could see little could be done. Then Hripsime saw a hand of a woman sticking up out of the rubble and she ran to it crawling desperately over the rocky debris and rebar that stuck up through it all. The husband was directly behind her and by the time they reached the arm with its tightly clinched fist, the husband was ahead of her picking up the first large block of crooked cement. Another man, who had also come upon the scene, motioned for Hripsime to stay back. As they picked up one blood spattered piece of rubble after another, Hripsime stood there in shock, praying. The duo worked frantically for several minutes until they realized there was only an arm that had been severed at the shoulder. The husband carried the arm to one side of the rubble to an uncluttered piece of ground. Then Hripsime watched as the husband tried to unclench the fist and soon a small hand inside of it was exposed. Hripsime, horrified at the sight, felt overwhelmed with grief.

When the husband and Hripsime came away and started back toward her building, he said, "I am pretty sure this was the mother and her daughter that lived in the flat next to us."

"I cannot imagine a more terrible way to die," she said.

"They must have been killed instantly," the husband responded with much emotion.

She knew he only wanted to comfort her. She also knew that this was something she should never have seen and that this would be a remembrance that would be with her always.

Hripsime could feel the strain of the moment amongst those that had gathered there. Mixed emotions brought about a muddled mind full of confusion. She was sad about the mother and her daughter, but thankful at the same time that God had spared this family once again. She did not see them after that, even though she knew they had set up housekeeping in another part of the same building, a part that was still standing.

The husband justified this by saying, "It is more likely that lightning will not strict twice in the same spot and I know now more than before the Lord will keep us safe."

As the bombs and the bullets continued throughout one particularly harsh day, her thoughts again dwelt on this family. Then Hripsime's mind carried her to the day she found out her brother might still be alive. She recalled how harried her thoughts had become as she thought about the reality that someone else from her family might have survived the terrible holocaust.

Although they both had been very young and it had been so long ago, she now tried to recall her brother. Still, his image did not materialize as she might have liked. His face in particular was unrecognizable. She had been without anyone for so long it seemed surreal to her as if she was only dreaming that she might have a brother out there somewhere.

Hripsime was in the schoolyard at the Armenian Evangelical School when one of the other teachers handed her a small magazine that had come from an orphanage in Jerusalem. Full of long lists of boys' names ages twelve and under, she could not set the magazine down until she had read it cover to cover. At the end of the lists, an ad caused her much emotional heaviness.

"Anyone who is related to one of these boys can come and pick him up, whether he would be a nephew, a son, a brother, it does not matter what kind of relationship you may have with them. Please come."

Hripsime carefully checked each name on the many lists with her finger. Gliding it down each page, her eyes focused suddenly on one with her family name. Shock filled her mind and she had to look away from it for a few minutes. Then her eyes clicked back as if drawn by a magnet and they steadied on the name, Luther Aghnoghian. At once, she wrote a letter, and sent it to the principal of the orphanage in Jerusalem, asking for more information. Soon she received a return letter. It told the story of the plight of the boys that were at that particular orphanage and Hripsime found it hard to read it in one sitting. She would read a little, put the letter away, then pull it out and then read a little more. By the time she finished reading it, she finally knew without a doubt that one of these boys was her brother.

At the end of the First World War, the English government had sent special, brave young men all over, mostly into the Syrian Desert. They had begun to realize that this was where many Armenians had been exiled, as they gradually uncovered more about the horrible deportation. Although they had been driven like cattle into the desert to die, rumors had reached them that some may have survived. Therefore, these men went around searching for Armenian boys. These young Englishmen would put on clothing to look like the Bedouins who lived under tents and moved around according to the weather. It was very shocking to her to find that so many Armenian boys had been living with the Bedouins, because they had the reputation of being a ruthless sort of people. These Englishmen were very smart in not letting anyone know their intentions. In different ways they found many of them with various families, as many had been taken by the Turks as servants or slaves. When found they took them to Jerusalem and kept them at the orphanage where they were fed and clothed for some time. Hripsime prayed that this was her brother, but still, doubts crept into her thoughts. How could she be certain?

Hripsime then wrote a letter to the boy whose name was Luther and asked if he could remember the names of his parents. In this way, she could make sure that he was really her brother.

The answer to this letter came from the principal. In it, she replied, "This boy was here, but now he has gone to Addis-Ababa, the Capital of Ethiopia. When Haile-Selassie, the Emperor of Ethiopia, came to pay a visit to the Holy City of Jerusalem, all the boys went to meet him, each one with his own primitive musical instrument to honor His Majesty. He was so delighted he asked if he could chose forty of them to take with him and we permitted him to choose and your brother was one of them. This was a good thing as we were no longer able to keep them due to a shortage of finances. Even now we are faced with having to close the orphanage all together, which means we will unfortunately have to scatter the remaining boys."

When Hripsime wrote Luther in Addis-Ababa and finally found him, her heart felt as if it might explode with joy. Hripsime learned later that during the time he was in the orphanage, Luther and the others boys were asked if they wanted to change their names and many did for many reasons. However, when her brother was specifically asked if he would like to change his German name Luther and have an Armenian name, he told them, "It is impossible for me to change my name, which was given to me by my dear parents whom I lost some years ago."

In one of his first letters he wrote his story about how he barely escaped when he was just a small boy of only seven years. Hripsime could not hold the tears back, as she read his words. This letter touched her so deeply she was shaken for several days.

"One day," Luther began writing, "during the deportation of Armenians, the savage Moslem gendarmes, that mercilessly had been driving our whole group like cattle, separated the children from the parents. They drove us in another direction corralling me along with other young boys and girls in a large stable where we all spent the night. We lay among the many animals anywhere we could find a little space to lie down; there were so many of us. The next morning, I awoke early and went away from the stable. I started walking in the direction I last saw my mother and father driven away hoping I could find them. I walked and walked and walked until it was dark. At last, I saw a light in the distance. As I walked toward it, I realized I was approaching a settlement of some kind. It looked like many tents of various sizes. Some dogs started to bark. One of them ran and lunged at me. Viciously it attacked me, biting me in several places on my body. I remember the pain and falling to the ground crying until I must have blacked out. I later learned that when the dogs saw my motionless body on the ground, they left me alone. I lay there the whole of that cold night, blood running from my wounds.

"The next morning a woman from the village of tents saw me and took me to her tent carrying me on her back. She washed my wounds and did whatever she knew best for me and I recovered somehow. I lived with this family for awhile. I am not sure how long. I helped them in any way I could. One day her husband took me along to his vegetable garden. It was a very hot day. We worked for some time. Then he told me to keep awake and watch that no one would come along and take any of the vegetables, while he napped under a shady tree. I sat there and tried very hard to keep my eyes open. Then all of a sudden a young man came with his donkey, trampled the vegetables, and then passed on by. It all happened so quickly I could do nothing.

"When the man awoke and saw his garden trampled down, he became furious with me and took a gun in his hand and told me, 'Go stand over there!' He aimed his gun at me and said, 'I am going to kill you!'

I remember trembling with such a tremendous fear that I felt I might die from just being so afraid. It seemed as if I was going to die for sure and so I shut my eyes and waited for the bullet to enter my body.

At that exact moment, a woman was passing by. When she saw the man pointing a gun at me, she ran toward me, and took a hold of my hand. Then we started to run as fast as we could.

She shouted at the man as we ran and said, 'Why are you killing this nice boy?'

I felt certain she was an angel sent from heaven to save my life."

As Hripsime thought about Luther's angel, a verse came to mind:

> For He shall give his angels charge over thee, to
> keep thee in all thy ways. (Psalm 91:11)

Hripsime continued to read Luther's letter, but she had to choke back the tears. Now and again, the words would blur and she would have to stop to dry her eyes.

"I lived with this woman's family for some time until the English came and delivered many of us Armenian boys from the

Bedouins. They took us to the orphanage in Jerusalem. Although it was a life of uncertainties, I was very grateful."

Luther and Hripsime found out later that all the other children who had been put in that large stable had been killed in different ways. Hripsime often thought about how if her brother had not woken up early that morning and walked away to find their mother and father, he would have been killed as well. And, if Luther would have changed his name, as many did, she would never have found him then.

Another miracle, Hripsime thought.

Hripsime prayed after she finished reading the letter. She could not thank God enough. He had saved her and now her brother from sure death. She also prayed that He might open a way for her to go and see Luther one day.

She treasured Luther's letters. They corresponded continually through the years. Once he wrote about how he had gotten a good job in a big Armenian shoe factory and became the top treasurer with a very good wage.

When he first met the owner, he tested Luther because he only had two years of elementary education. The owner gave him the account book of the factory. It was a mess, full of errors. The test was that he had to find the errors and correct them. Luther took the ledger and worked hard on it. Finally finding all the errors, he corrected them in such a way that the owner could not believe it.

He asked him, "Who did this?" and Luther said, "I did it." Surprised at Luther's inborn ability and talent, the owner said, "You can manage the whole business."

After some time passed, Luther married and had a family. Every piece of correspondence, especially the snapshots he sent were like precious treasures from heaven to Hripsime. Sometimes a gift would arrive and when she would gaze upon it, it was as if it were the first appearance of manna on the desert floor. However, as time went along there was never an opportunity for them to see one another. Still, Hripsime prayed daily for this as the years rolled along. Addis-Ababa was a great distance away and at times it seemed to Hripsime this city was on the other side of the world.

– Five –

Hripsime was lying silently in her bed as she listened to the quiet of her building, and more importantly, the quiet in the streets of the Christian Quarter. This heightened her attentiveness. Beirut had not been this quiet even before the war started. There had been a few moments of peaceful consideration these past few weeks, but nothing like this and she feared the worse, that the enemy was up to something. She knew they would not stop until they were all dead. This was the way of things in Lebanon during these times. A peaceful coexistence was not in the thinking of some in this world and most of all not in the mind of a Muslim. This is what she had learned more than anything else while she endured the Turkish wars in her youth. This is the way it was and she imagined this is the way it would always be until Jesus comes back.

Then she thought about what it would be like to have no one to talk to, no one to love, and no one to talk to about Jesus. The loneliness she felt at that moment gnawed at her insides. It seemed to her she was the only one in the world. For some time, this lonely feeling stayed with her and controlled her every thought. Gradually, her mind carried her back into the past again, as she began to recall some of the more special times with her children and her husband. Tears began to well up from deep inside and spill out over the rims of her eye lids, as she thought about that moment when God had shown her the man she was to marry. And, again, she thought about that most important moment when she accepted Jesus into her life.

At the Armenian Evangelical School where she taught, the janitor, or janitress, a woman in charge of cleaning the school building, was like a mother to her. One evening she invited Hripsime to go to a revival meeting, which was close to the school. With some coaxing, Hripsime decided to go. However, after the first meeting, she attended several more. One night after the meeting, she came home and read the whole Gospel of John in one night and it became very clear to her that just being a good person with her own righteousness was not good enough to obtain eternal life.

One verse especially caught her attention:

> For God so loved the world that he gave his only
> begotten son that whosoever believeth in him
> should not perish, but have everlasting life.
> (John 3:16)

As she read this particular verse over and over, it occurred to her, only the blood of Jesus shed on the cross of Calvary would wash her clean and make her worthy of eternal life. Then and there she fell to her knees and prayed aloud to God and invited Jesus Christ to come into her heart and have full dominion over all things in her life. The assurance of salvation thrilled her so much she became full to overflowing with the joy of it and a peace flooded her mind she did not understand.

Eventually, it became impossible to keep this joy within her. While walking back and forth to school, she felt as if she were flying. She wanted to tell everyone she met in the streets about the love of God, about how He had sent His Son to die on the cross for her sins.

When they asked her at one of the revival meetings to give her testimony, she leaped at the chance. On that same night, a man of God, Mihran Kassarjian, was sitting in the gathering. Hripsime would learn later that he was a college graduate and a teacher also from Turkey, but that most of all he was an evangelist. Later, she would learn that his ministry consumed most of his time. Always striving for the most effective way to reach out to others for Jesus, his obsession drove him from dawn to well into a night, with all other things classified as a hindrance or nuisance to him.

Mihran told her after they met that when he heard her testimony, he went directly home to tell his eighty-two-year-old father, the Reverent Kevork Kassarjian, who was a retired pastor after fifty-five years. Although bedridden for a long time, he almost jumped from his bed when his son told him he had met the girl he wanted to marry. His father had been waiting anxiously to see at least one of his sons wed before he passed away. When Mihran told his unmarried older brother and sister, the four of them prayed about it. Marriage indeed, during these times, was a family affair.

A day did not go by that Mihran's father did not try to sway him about getting married. However, Mihran was so involved in the Lord's work that it seemed he neither had the time nor the desire for marriage. This was hard for Hripsime to understand in the beginning, but later, when she realized how deep his dedication was to the Lord, she grew to understand his ways and learned not to take it personally.

One day, Hripsime's janitor friend, the woman who had invited her to that first revival meeting, asked her to go with her to see Mihran's father. She had sewn a nightgown for him and wanted to give it to him. Her friend went up to his room alone, which was on the roof, while Hripsime waited in the yard below. After some time passed, her friend called to her and she went up to meet the old pastor. As soon as he saw her, he told Hripsime she was the woman for his son. Later Hripsime was told about how they had all prayed about this whole matter.

Mihran's sister, Lucy, a child of God, came to visit Hripsime every now and then in the school yard to persuade her to marry Mihran. Overwhelmed by it all, Hripsime could not be convinced. Maybe if she had had more contact with Mihran and he had not been so distant during those beginning days, her decision might have been different, but as it was Hripsime had other plans. What was uppermost in her thoughts was to study nursing. She had an invitation to teach that next year, but she had grown tired of teaching. Becoming a nurse had now become the main thrust in her life with everything else at a different level.

At that time, she was living in a small room very close to the school and felt exhausted after a day of teaching from 8:00 until 4:00, with only a short break at noon. Constantly on her feet, talking, explaining, teaching and then coming home with a big pile of copy books to correct, usually sixty in number, became too grueling for any young girl and desperately, she craved some spare time. Also, there was the time it took just to prepare a meal. Living alone she had no one to help her and in those days when there was no icebox, no ready made canned food, no facility of any sort, each day fresh food had to be bought and cooked and this consumed much time. Therefore, her passion for nursing grew in her heart and she soon found herself making full plans to make the leap into such a career. Never before had she been this certain as to exactly what she wanted for her life.

When she applied to the Nursing School at the American University of Beirut, the principal, Miss Vanzant, an American lady, was more than glad to know that a college graduate was coming into the school. Many who applied did not know English and there was no time to teach these students a foreign language; therefore, Hripsime's knowledge of English also elated Miss

Vanzant. Without hesitation, she sent Hripsime the nursing school catalog and she made arrangements for a health certificate. Now Hripsime was ready in every way to leave for Beirut, but classes did not begin for several more weeks.

All at the same time, she had invitations for her old job teaching, for the nursing school, and the possible marriage to Mihran that was still being considered by his family. All of this pressed her to the limit. She really had no intention of getting married, but with the three matters at hand, she started to pray day and night to God that He would reveal His will in her life.

Her pillow would be wet with tears every night as this struggle went on inside of her for some time. Deep down in her heart she knew God wanted her to marry this man even though he was twenty years her senior. Yet, no clear answer came and now time was growing short.

One afternoon, Hripsime entered a small room in the school building and she knelt and prayed with all of her heart for an immediate answer. At the end of her prayer, God gave her a song to sing and in Armenian she sang the words, "Lord, whatever is your will, let it be my will also. I am now willing to do Thy will."

As she strolled along, she sang this tune with its unusual words aloud as if it were bursting from her heart. Unbeknownst to Hripsime, that same afternoon, at the same time, Mihran's family, the four, had been praying as well. Finally, they came to the decision that this would be the last time for them to ask her to marry him. If her answer was no, then they would ask and pray about it no more.

As she was coming out of the room, singing the song with the words, "Thy will be done," Mihran's sister, Lucy, was coming toward her from the opposite direction and heard her singing. When they sat down on a bench, she told Hripsime that this was her last visit and that they would not ask her again. However, as they talked, it was very plain to both of them that this was God's will. Nevertheless, it was now up to Hripsime to decide. When the word "yes" came forth, it surprised her a little, but not really. No one else, only her Heavenly Father, to whom she had committed her life could have persuaded her.

After several months, Hripsime and Mihran married in September of 1926. They carried her father-in-law to the ceremony in a wheelchair. It was late summer and many of the Armenian pastors were out of town on vacation, therefore, the President of the Aleppo College for Boys did the ceremony, but in a very strange American way, Hripsime thought.

This very distinguished gentleman blurted out, "If anyone here has an objection, let him speak it now. If not, he is to keep his or her mouth shut afterwards."

After the ceremony, they knelt down in front of Mihran's father and the old pastor put his hands on their heads and blessed them with a very cheerful heart. Obviously, he had been waiting for this hour a long time. He lived three months after their wedding day and then passed away to be with the Lord on Christmas Day, something he had prayed would happen.

God gave Mihran and Hripsime four beautiful children. The first, Marie, was born in 1927. Joel's arrival was also in 1927. Many years before their marriage, God had come to Mihran in a dream and promised him a son and that his name should be Joel, one of the Minor Prophets. George was the next, born in 1933, and then Barkev in 1935. All were born in Aleppo, Syria.

Their family life was not easy. On a limited income with four children, an unmarried brother-in-law and a sister-in-law, the meals were meager, but they learned to expect the bare necessities. Mihran was deep into his evangelism, but he squeaked out enough time to be a part-time teacher, teaching English and French at a Moslem College. Although, they went through hard times financially, the Lord never let them down and they always had enough. She was always amazed each month that they were able to stretch their income to the end.

Hripsime then remembered one of her favorite promises she had clung to all these years, a promise she claimed for herself:

I will not fail thee, nor forsake thee. (Joshua 1:5)

For Mihran, living by God's promises was more of an automatic thing. Always she had felt God had given him a larger portion of faith than he had given her. However, as time went along it was through Mihran, Hripsime felt God had deepened her faith and had drawn her much closer to Him, her Lord and Savior.

"Praise the Lord," she said, all at once, as she thought about how she loved the Lord with her whole heart, mind and soul and about the strength He gave her each day to live in Him.

– Six –

The shelling had started again. Hripsime's building rumbled, creaked and moaned from the strain of it all. When one blast came so close it shook everything in her flat and plaster fell from the ceiling, she dropped to the floor and covered her head.

This is the end of things on earth anyway, she thought.

Anything breakable had been boxed away long ago, especially the pictures that used to hang on the walls that now looked like road maps. She had saved only a few dishes and they could break, if that was God's will. Lately, she had avoided, at all costs, venturing any distance from her fourth-floor flat, the smell from the garbage and the carnage in the streets was unbearable. Once in awhile she would take a look from her balcony, but it was a sickening sight. In all directions, most buildings on the narrow street below were nothing more than bombed out shells, which teetered or tilted in a terrifying way. The blackened, scorched bricks and mortar from the gunpowder of the blasts of bombs caused the Christian sector to look like a ghost town, but in an eerie sort of way.

She imagined most were dead or had escaped in some miraculous way and she knew she was one of the few noncombatants who remained in Beirut. As she looked out through her tears, the sight of it all caused her to think of Aleppo, Syria and another war, World War II.

During the first part of the war, Hripsime and Mihran tried to stay clear of what was happening. However, after the Vichy, a tool used by the Nazis, left in late 1942, things calmed down and many soldiers came to Aleppo, from England, Ireland, New Zealand and Australia. Because of this, the Salvation Army was able to send a captain to Aleppo to open a canteen for these soldiers. When Mihran and Hripsime heard they were having Gospel meetings on Sunday afternoons, they became very interested and wanted to participate in some way.

Before the war, Mihran had written to the Salvation Army asking them if it would be possible to come to Syria and proclaim the Good News of salvation. They wrote back and explained they would come with pleasure to Syria, but the Syrian Government had forbidden such a venture. However, now the government was not able to stop them because they had vowed to serve the soldiers who had come to fight.

The Syrian population was more than ninety percent Arabs, the overwhelming majority being of the Sunni Moslem religion; however other sects were represented: the Ismailis, the Shiites, and the Alawites, a branch of the Shiites. These were Muslims that practiced their own faith. The largest non-Arab minorities were the Kurds, a pastoral people, who concentrated along the Turkish border. There were only a small number of Armenian Christians, who were either of the Greek or Armenian Orthodox tradition, and too, a handful of Jewish were represented. Mihran usually geared his evangelism toward this small number of Turkish speaking people, as the Muslims were generally hard to reach.

Therefore, when the soldiers came to Aleppo, he gladly welcomed this whole new ministry.

As soon as Mihran and Hripsime heard the revival meetings had started, they attended. One Sunday afternoon, after the meeting, they met with the captain and introduced themselves.

"We are more than glad for these gospel meetings and we want to encourage you to keep on spreading the Good News," Mihran said.

Then Hripsime asked the captain if there might be a job for her and he said he would pray about it. The next day, the captain sent news that he needed a cashier and a manager and asked if she wanted to work at the canteen in this way. Even though the pay was small, she was delighted that she could have such a job as this during these hard times and she started working immediately.

Many soldiers came and stood in line to be served eggs, chips, bread, butter and tea. There was so much order and discipline, she thought; always, they waited patiently for their turn to be served. As she became more acquainted, she was surprised at how many believers were among them, but also there were many who were not believers. She and Mihran began inviting several to come to their home to have what they called "cottage meetings." They sang, prayed, and many gave their testimonies. Also, there were many who had never heard the Good News before and there were many among these that became believers. The compassion and heaviness Hripsime felt for these men was fierce as most were headed to a frontline somewhere and their chances of survival were slim.

Hripsime felt God had preserved their family in many ways during this war. They all seemed immune to the dangers that befell Aleppo. During the whole of the war, because their little house was located right next to the Aleppo Railroad Station, it was under constant attack. The enemy shelled the tracks and station continually because this kind of target was of major importance to the allies and to the enemy. Pieces of bombs and fragments of the buildings bombarded the roof of their house on a regular basis, but God spared them during these hard times.

This too was another miracle, Hripsime thought.

Towards the end of the war, Joel, their eldest son, was drafted, and served in the infantry of the Syrian Army. One day, while running an errand near the border, a buried bomb exploded under his motorbike. When the front wheel touched that precarious spot, the bomb detonated and the concussion threw him and his bike to the other side of the road into an open field. Because it was late in the evening and the night descended quickly, it was not long before it grew pitch-black. With no houses in the vicinity, no one happened onto the scene. Joel lay there on the hard ground unconscious the entire night as if dead. Anything could have happened, but did not. Prevalent were many predator type animals and insects: wild animals, snakes, birds of prey, scorpions and more. However, God covered him and kept him under His wings.

Hripsime now thought about a particular Psalm, but with much more reverence than ever before.

…He will cover you with His pinions and under

His wings you may seek refuge. (Psalm 91:4)

The next morning, when an army car passed by, the driver was shocked to see an army bike on the road. At once he looked around to try to find the operator of the bike. Finally, he found a tall young boy on the other side of the road. At first sight, he thought he was dead; however, as he drew closer, he found that the boy was still breathing, but barely. He carried him to his car and drove him to the army hospital where he was treated for three months. After some time passed, when Joel felt better, he wrote a few lines to his parents.

"I was dead, but now I am alive because of God's wonderful mercy and because I know you both had been praying."

This was truly another miracle, Hripsime thought, and she praised God for the way He had brought her son to Him.

Marie, Hripsime's daughter, started high school at the beginning of the war and graduated shortly before it ended. In 1948, she met a physician, Henry Badeer in their home and they married in Beirut July 12 that same year. Shortly afterwards Henry and Marie went to Boston in America, so Henry could spend a year in research at Harvard on a Rockefeller Fellowship. When they returned, they settled in Beirut and Gilbert was born in December of 1949. Their second son, Daniel, was born in March 1954.

After the war, Joel, George and Barkev, along with Aunt Lucy, continued to live at home in Aleppo while George and Barkev completed their schooling.

Hripsime served with the Salvation Army until the end of the war. When the canteen closed, she asked the captain to give her a recommendation, which he gladly did. He wrote how she had served them faithfully and that any employer should not hesitate to hire her. He also recommended that Hripsime be given only the best and highest position that anyone could give her. With that recommendation in hand, she went directly to a private hospital where many Armenian physicians practiced medicine. Owned by a famous Armenian surgeon, Dr. Altounyan, she showed him this recommendation. After reading it, he plunged the letter into his pocket and ran quickly to the matron of the hospital telling her, "Here is the lady we have been looking for our hospital."

Hripsime started to work immediately as a general supervisor of all the workers. She also managed the store and the housekeeping. Hripsime loved her work at the hospital. She was not a nurse, but the next best thing. One of her favorites about her job was managing the nurses and teaching them English. Few knew English and since the nursing courses were all taught in English, this was a tremendous asset to the hospital. Above all else, there were many opportunities to witness and to make a difference with those that were ill. Hripsime saw many of God's miracles during the ten years she worked there and she was very grateful that He had used her in this way.

One time while she was working at the hospital, Dr. Altounyan asked her to pay a visit to another hospital in another town, a Danish hospital. Because they were Danish nurses governed by an English system, she was to examine if their way was a better way of running a hospital.

On a Sunday morning, with the doctor's own car and driver, they drove many hours to the town of this hospital. It took two days for her to observe their ways. When the driver returned to pick her up, she gave him her locked suitcase to put on the roof in a baggage rack. They had driven into the night and it was dark when they arrived at the hospital. Hripsime was very tired. When the driver went to retrieve her suitcase and discovered it was gone, the shock of it overwhelmed her as almost everything she owned was in it including her Bible. Silently, with much despair, she walked off toward her home. She said nothing to her husband and family, but went directly to bed.

The next morning, Mihran noticed that she looked gloomy and asked, "What is wrong with you? You look so sad."

"My suitcase is lost. Somewhere on the way back it must have fallen from the rack."

Mihran, a man of great faith, acted as if this was nothing and said, in a very easy manner, "Don't worry, we will pray and it will be found."

He was always teaching her a better way to trust in the Lord and this was probably one of those times; however, this time she just laughed, as she could not believe that the suitcase, which was lost on a long road between the two towns, would ever be found.

After several days, a girl from the hospital was walking in the market to do some shopping. She heard two men talking about a suitcase that they had found on the road that went out of town and one of them said, "I opened it, but there was no money in it just some feminine items and a Bible. This surely is a sign that the owner must be a righteous woman, so we must find this woman and give it to her."

The next day, the girl came to meet Hripsime at the gate of the hospital. As Hripsime entered the gate, the girl shouted to her.

"Mrs. Kassarjian! Your suitcase has been found!"

"What! Are you serious?"

"No, no, come with me and I will show you."

Hripsime then followed the young girl to the shop in the market and asked the man if he had found a suitcase. At first he was a little bit cross and he asked if she could tell him every item that had been in it. When she told him about its contents, his expression changed.

"I am sure you are the owner," he said, and he handed her the suitcase.

"Thank you from the bottom of my heart. God is wonderful," Hripsime said.

While she was returning home to tell her husband and her family, her heart leaped with joy. She was thankful to her Heavenly Father who had heard their prayers and answered them in such a short time.

Here's yet another miracle, Hripsime thought, as she fondly recalled her husband's undoubting faith. Through this experience, she learned that God truly does care about even the smaller things.

Shortly after this, Hripsime fell seriously ill and needed major surgery. Dr. Altounyan, who did the surgery, said there was no hope for her and that she would not survive.

While she was on the operating table, just before they gave her an anesthetic, she prayed and said within her heart, "Dear Heavenly Father, Almighty God, I commit my body, soul and spirit into Your hands. I also commit all the physicians and nurses into Your hands. Nothing is impossible for You as you have told me in Jeremiah 32:27. I need your wonderful, miraculous power in this present situation, Lord, as you have shown Thy wonderful power in different times in my life. Even in a hopeless situation like this, if you can find a suitcase, Lord, surely this little operation is not too much for you. In the precious name of Jesus, I pray. Amen."

Dr. Altournyan worked on her for over five hours, from nine in the morning until two o'clock that afternoon. She required many blood transfusions before, during and after the operation. Miraculously, the hospital was able to obtain enough units of Hripsime's rare blood type. Dr. Altournyan cut...and God healed.

And, again, another miracle needed to be counted among the many others, she thought.

She stayed at the hospital for a whole month and because she was one of them, all of the staff and nurses treated her with extra care. However, when she finally went home, she went home never to return to her dear friends and to the job she loved so much. And, so it happened that another door closed in Hripsime's life, but she knew another one would open soon.

With her heart fully open to God, she felt more peace and contentment than ever before; God had saved her in a more personal way. She knew that he loved her and obviously he wanted her to continue on in some way.

— Seven —

Several weeks now had passed since the first bombs had fallen. Sometimes there was electricity and the phone might have worked, but most of the time these things were not expected. On one blessed day, however, Hripsime's phone did ring. The shock caused her to stand still like a stone statue as she listened in disbelief to its chime; it had not rung for a very long time. Then she could not get to it fast enough. Its ring blocked out every other sound and thought until she finally picked up the receiver.

"Auntie?"

"Yes," Hripsime cried out. It had been so long since she had talked to any of her loved ones and her eyes grew misty with happiness. This was her niece, her brother's daughter, whom she had not heard from in a long time.

"Auntie, we have decided to escape from Beirut. Are you willing to come with us?"

"Yes, I think so," Hripsime said. "You don't know how good it is to hear from someone. Do you know anything about Joel, his wife and the two little ones? I have heard nothing."

"Yes, Auntie. We just learned that they were able to escape through a friend and they're in Iran with Barkev and Cathy and their daughter. I know they have been worried for you Auntie but they could not reach you, West Beirut was much worse than East Beirut where you are, Auntie."

Hripsime's heart soared when she heard her son and his family were safe. Now she could leave with no question. Then she thought about her prayer and how she had asked God to find an escape for Joel and his family and for herself as well.

"I had no idea they had made it safely. There have been no lines of communication here. In fact, I am surprised I am talking to you this moment."

"I know Auntie. It has been the same for us too. So, are you going with us?"

"Yes. I am more than willing to go," Hripsime said.

In the back of her mind, she was already planning what to do with her furniture, but she was hoping too she could take some of her things with her.

"May I bring a few things?"

"Yes, but try to make it two suitcases or bundles."

"What will you do with all your new furniture? You just finished furnishing your place."

"We were hesitant in the beginning because of this, but the other day a bomb hit our building and part of it collapsed. We've been living in the basement for several days now: sitting, eating and sleeping on the hard stone stairs. What good is furniture when you can't use it and it will probably be blown to pieces anyway," her niece cried. "I can't believe it, Auntie. I can't believe what's happening."

"Because there is a cease-fire, my husband is going to the seashore to one of the boat owners and try to make arrangements for us today. Stay safe and my husband will be there to get you very soon."

"I will be ready, dear one," Hripsime said, as she hung up the phone to her life line.

While she tried to think about what to do first, she sank down into one of the straight back chairs. Staring out into the smoky sky, she noticed the building across the way was near to collapsing. She took a sip of coffee from a cup she had just poured before the phone rang and paused briefly as she thought about the bitter taste it left in her mouth. It had been too long since she had had a fresh cup of coffee with grounds that were straight from a can. She had reused these particular grounds too many times, but was thankful she had them, as she thought back to the times when there had been no coffee or any kind of food.

Then Hripsime recalled the time she had a cup of coffee with several ladies at the Palace Hotel in Cairo, Egypt. This was a very special time when she was on her way to visit her brother and his family. This would be the first time she had seen him since he was a toddler on her father's shoulders.

A year after she left the hospital, in 1954, the same year Barkev left for America, an unexpected letter arrived from her brother. In it was a round-trip ticket for her to travel to Addis-Ababa. They were small children when they had lost each other and now there was much in her head about what it would be like to see him and his family. Her excitement bubbled up and out of her like bubbling water over the rim of a boiling pot. She could hardly wait. Impatience captured every thought she tried to produce.

From Aleppo, she flew to Beirut to stay with her daughter, Marie, her husband, Henry, and her two grandsons. For several days, she waited to hear from the airline. When the good news came, she departed at once, with Marie and Henry driving her to the airport. They embraced one another as if she would be gone forever.

After some nervous hustle and bustle, she settled down into her seat next to a window. It was a small plane. In those days there were no big planes to Ethiopia, but she knew nothing of such things. This was the first time she had ever flown. She knew she should be nervous, but the nervousness of meeting her brother outweighed any fear she might have had about flying.

The first stop was Cairo where she stayed in a very large hotel, the Palace Hotel. Awe stricken everywhere she looked, its elegant one hundred and fifty rooms truly made it seem like a palace. Before she went up to her room, she sent a cable to her brother, giving him the flight number and the time of her arrival. She wanted to be sure it would reach him in time, as the flight would be late coming into Addis-Ababa the next day on Sunday.

After she found her room and experienced her first elevator ride, she had dinner in one of the most beautiful dinning rooms she had ever seen. Later in the evening, she sat at a large table in an adjoining yard. Thirty American tourist ladies gathered around her and seemed to be very interested in her. They were on their way to Africa, which struck Hripsime as strange. She had never encountered tourist people before. It had never occurred to her to travel for the mere pleasure of traveling. However, as the evening went along, she found the ladies interesting as several were from America. After Hripsime met each one, they talked for some time while she sipped on some of the best coffee she had ever tasted. With absolutely no bitterness, the taste of a very aromatic bean caused her to swoon with much delight.

"Where are you traveling to?" one particular lady asked.

"I am traveling to Addis-Ababa. It is the Capitol of Ethiopia."

"How interesting. What is there to see in Addis-Ababa?"

"I am to meet my brother there who has been lost to me for forty years now," Hripsime said.

A tear began to roll down her cheek, but quickly she wiped it away with the back of her hand for fear one of the ladies might notice. Then an unexpected excitement roared through the group of ladies and they wanted her to tell them more of herself.

"We've never met anyone before who has gone through these kinds of experiences," one lady said.

As Hripsime relayed several brief events in her life, one of the ladies rose up from her chair, walked over to Hripsime and warmly hugged her. And, then the others joined in, as well. Soon all were hugging and kissing her and mixing their tears with hers.

After a restless night with little sleep, the morning seemed particularly strained. Her anxiousness to meet her brother and the strange scenery about her caused her much uneasiness. On the plane, she wished the ladies were with her, but now she was alone again. Only a few were on the plane and no one was sitting next to her. The strangeness that surrounded her consumed her thoughts, however, her enthusiasm still ran high because this was the last leg of her trip and soon she would be with her brother.

Later that evening, at seven o'clock, when the plane touched down at the Addis-Ababa Airport, Hripsime's nerves wanted to jump from her body. As the passengers disembarked, a heavy rain was flooding the tarmac as they hurried toward the terminal. Her shoes and stockings were soaked by the time she reached the door that was being held open by an airline attendant.

She followed nervously behind the others, as they hurried along a passageway that led to a cavernous room of disorderly lines of people and heaping bags of luggage. On a huge sign sprawled across the entrance to the room was the word "Customs" in large Arabic letters. Here, confusion reigned. Black officers speaking different languages were searching every suitcase. Not one white man was among them. Her heart beat faster and faster as she came closer and closer to the head of the line, where they were ransacking people and any bag they might have hanging from them. She was the last one in line, so all of this had a lot of time to play with her mind. In vain, she looked around to see if she could catch a glimpse of her brother, but only the black faces loomed out at her. She watched them intently as they individually searched each passenger and she tried to imagine what it was going to feel like when it came to be her turn. She had great misgivings about someone touching her like this even if it was for security reasons. Her heart was pounding in her ears. A terrible dread was building up with much anxiety as she neared the black men.

This being in a foreign country, among foreign people, who speak in such a strange way, and with such force is a horrible thing, she thought.

"Oh, Lord, help me," she whispered so no one else could hear.

Then suddenly she was through it; she had cleared customs and she had not even remembered what had happened. Hripsime then retreated to a corner with her luggage and dropped down on her suitcase exasperated with the whole situation. Her brother was no where in sight. The only way out was to cry out to Almighty God, she thought, and she poured out her whole heart to Him for help and direction.

Then his promise in Psalm 50:12 came to mind as she prayed and softly quoted this verse verbatim:

> Call unto me in the day of trouble and I shall
> rescue you and you will honor me. (Psalm 50:12)

Directly after she finished this prayer, she looked around and saw a young man, with a lighter complexion than some of the others. She picked up her suitcase and approached him. It was as if God were leading her to him and she asked the man, "Do you speak English?"

"Who are you? Why are you asking me if I speak English?" he said in English.

She decided she must have startled him by suddenly approaching him and asking such a question. Then she asked, not knowing really why she asked such a thing, "Are you Armenian?"

"Why are you asking me all these questions? What do you want? Why have you come to me?" he responded, with an even more surprised look upon his face.

Not able to control her emotions, a tear rolled down her cheek.

"I have come to meet my brother whom I lost forty years ago. Do you know him? His name is Luther Aghnoghian," she said.

As soon as the man heard Luther's name, the expression on his face changed and his tone softened as he said, "Yes."

When she heard the word yes, she could not contain herself and she shouted with much joy from deep inside of her, "Praise the Lord."

She had totally forgotten where she was and had not considered the people around her in her excitement. Sheepishly she began to look around to see if anyone had heard her little outburst. Although these were all strange people, she knew she was among mostly Muslims. However, when she saw no real harm had been down, she gathered her composure and began to focus on her new found help. The man had cooled down considerably and was now responding to her questions.

"Yes, I am an Armenian. Luther is my colleague and we are in the same business."

Once again, without thinking, the words came out, "Praise the Lord." However, this time she did not care who heard her, she just wanted to hug her new friend whom God speedily had brought her.

Indeed, this is another miracle, she thought.

Then she boldly asked, "Can you take me to my brother?"

"I am here to meet a friend of mine, but fortunately he has not come, so I will drive you to your brother's house," he said.

"Praise the Lord!" Hripsime blurted out one more time.

The rain was still coming down in torrents. It coated the car as if it were under a waterfall. The man called it an autumn rain. Once settled, the man explained as he drove along that it was a long distance, and it did seem to Hripsime like an eternity before they reached her brother's house. She stayed in the car while Luther's friend went up to the door. The pouring rain had not diminished in any way and she noticed that Luther's friend was drenched as he stood out in the wet knocking on her brother's door.

"No one is at home. There is no light," he said when he returned. "I will check with the neighbors."

After knocking on the door of the next-door neighbor and on several other doors on down the row of houses, he returned to the car sloshing along with clothes so wet, Hripsime did not see how they could ever be dry again.

"We have to go to my house where I can change my clothes. We can rest awhile there and then we'll drive back again."

At his home, his Italian wife welcomed Hripsime in Italian and prepared a hot cup of tea for them all. He changed his clothes and after an hour they started out once again. The dreadful rain seemed like a permanent condition with no sign of ending. By the time they arrived the second time, it was nine o'clock. This time as they approached, they saw a light in the window. As they parked in front of Luther's house, her heart skipped a couple of beats. The anticipation of meeting her brother was almost too much for her.

Then Hripsime asked Luther's friend, "Please go in and say a guest is in the car, but don't tell him that his sister has come."

A smile spread across his face as he hopped out and headed for the house. Waiting patiently, fidgeting with the strap on her purse, her excitement intensified as each moment passed. Her thoughts, emotions and feelings were beyond anything that was explainable. When the door opened, she watched her brother as he stood in the doorway with the light to his back.

"I am sure it is my wife. Tell her to come in," her brother said.

Still she sat steadfast in the car with a tight grip on the handle of the door.

Then a sweet, young voice boomed from the background, "She must be my Auntie!"

Hripsime later grew to love this daughter of Luther's with an ever increasing passion. Her sweet smile always seemed to melt her heart no matter what they talked about or what they did together.

"No, this cannot be. She was to send a cable so we could meet her at the airport," Luther insisted.

Then they all came running out of the house and drew near to the car. They peered into the windows as if they were looking for a strange being from another planet. Her dear brother then opened the door and helped her out. He took her suitcase with one hand and held her hand with the other as they walked in the torrential rain on an uneven walkway made of stone. Neither of them said any words—they were speechless. All her tears had dried up. All her hankies were wet. When they entered the house, she put her arms around his neck, but still they could not talk. The situation seemed unreal, as if she were in a dream. She could not believe that she and her brother were together at last.

Her innermost thoughts climbed to the highest of heights and all she could think of was, *Praise God*, almost saying it aloud. Again, she thought, *this is yet another miracle.*

As the days went along with her brother and his family, it seemed like she was visiting heaven. The next day Luther's wife invited all of their friends and neighbors for a banquet. There was much food and much congeniality. She and Luther especially had a wonderful time shedding tears of joy and sorrow. They reminisced about their lost parents and recalled all their loved ones, but when the Armenian deportation was spoken of, a sorrow filled them both.

As the stay grew longer, a bigger sorrow filled Hripsime's heart, when she realized her brother was dead and not alive. Both he and his family were lost and had not been found by the miraculous, wonderful power of God, and so this saddened Hripsime very much. From that moment forward, Hripsime prayed for her brother and his family and for their salvation.

Hripsime stayed in Addis-Ababa with her brother for four months. She was very interested in hearing about his life and about his escape from certain death, when he escaped from the stable to the time he lived with the Bedouins in the tents.

However, as she met the many Armenian families in Addis-Ababa, she grieved. Although they had good positions, they had all lost interest in the church or in any Christian fellowship. She continually prayed for how she could somehow make a difference with this condition.

One day a lady asked, "Would you like to visit this woman whose husband is an old priest? He has been abed from an accident."

"With pleasure," Hripsime said, and soon not only this lady, but several ladies went with her to see the old priest's wife.

"I am so very glad to meet you. I have heard many things about you since you have arrived here in Addis-Ababa," the woman said.

Hripsime noticed a Bible beside her bed and when Hripsime picked it up, the priest's wife asked, "Would you read a little from it to me, please?"

"I will try," Hripsime said, being very careful to not appear too superior, as it was obvious she had more education than the others. Silence fell over the group as each listened with eager intent.

After several visits and as they became better acquainted, the same lady who asked her to visit the priest's wife asked Hripsime, "Could you lead us on a regular basis for we are all very hungry for the Word of God?"

"It would be my pleasure," Hripsime said, with a smile.

Inwardly she praised God for answering her prayers and for opening this door.

After this, once a week, they came together in one of their houses and they studied God's precious word. At first, a few of them came, but as time went along, more came. The studies were a smashing success and much joy flowed through the hearts of those who attended. When it came time for Hripsime to leave, there were over thirty ladies that were coming to the gatherings. They grieved about discontinuing these weekly meetings and she felt very sorry for them, but Hripsime knew she needed to return to her own family and her children who were waiting anxiously for her return.

The priest's wife seemed to recover somewhat and was able to sit in a chair from time to time. Hripsime helped her with some ideas in leading the group and she said that with God's help she would try to carry on with the study. She prayed that their numbers would expand as she knew the need was great in this starving community.

When she returned to her home in Aleppo and told Mihran about her visit, they both prayed. Her heart overflowed in thankfulness for the unique privilege to be with her long lost brother. She praised God for His wonderful mercy and grace for both of them to be alive and to meet each other. Most of all, she was thankful that God had used her to plant a seed in Addis-Ababa.

It weighed on her heart deeply that thousands and thousands of Armenian boys and girls had been mercilessly killed. She had heard that during those terrible years of deportation by the Turks, some were thrown into the rivers, others burned, others died of hunger, and many died of thirst and disease in the desert. The guilt that she survived when others had perished had always been very difficult for her to deal with. However, now she seemed better able to accept this heavy burden, since she had seen her brother and his family.

Hripsime began busying herself shuffling through the drawers of one of her chests in her fourth-floor flat. She had now come away from her recollections of her brother and was now thinking of another miracle. She realized, as she put many things into a garbage bag to give away, there was even more to be thankful for. Here was Luther's daughter coming to get her from this awful, inescapable situation. It was as if God had arranged her escape from Beirut forty years before when He brought her brother out of Turkey.

"Praise God!" she cried aloud. "This again is another miracle!"

Hripsime's knees buckled under her as she tried to understand what she could have done in her life to cause Him to single her out as one who was special. And, then she stopped trying to understand as she thought about Jesus and the cross. Then her favorite verse came to mind:

> For God so loved the world that he gave his only begotten Son, that whosoever believeth in him should not perish, but have everlasting life. (John 3:16)

– Eight –

Hripsime's niece called again that same day and explained, "Auntie, Nerses has been able to buy us passage on a small boat. This boat owner has taken many to Cyprus."

Hripsime could hardly respond. Tears streamed down her cheeks with no control. There was a rattle in her throat, as well, but finally the words came and she said, "I'll be ready dear one whenever you say."

All she could think of was that God had answered her prayers and that he wanted her to continue on in some way.

"Tomorrow, Auntie. Can you be ready by tomorrow?"

"Yes. I will be ready."

She had lived in that flat for twenty years so there was much to sift through and discard. With the help of God and the cease-fire, Hripsime was able to sell or give away several pieces of furniture including her bed, rugs, kitchen articles and a radio, and even though it was for a very low price, she felt more at ease thinking some one could use these things instead of leaving them to be blasted to pieces. What remained she gave away and many things she knew she would just have to leave, as she tried to pack up what meant the most to her.

With heavy emotions, she glanced through some pictures of her husband and children as she carefully packed them away into one of the suitcases she was taking with her. She fell back on a blanket on the floor that was now her make-shift bed and again her mind slipped back in time as she reminisced about the time just before she and her husband moved to Beirut.

Mihran's health was poor and he was anxious to move. He felt Hripsime should be nearer to their daughter in Beirut in case something happened to him. A special pang pushed against her chest; Hripsime would not only be near her daughter and son-in-law, but her two small grandsons as well.

In 1954, while they were still living in Aleppo, Barkev, their youngest son, left for the States. After Barkev graduated from high school, he desperately wanted to go to America to continue his education and to get a higher degree there. Therefore, Mihran wrote a letter to one of his old friends who had long ago gone to the States and asked him if he could help Barkev in any way. After some time passed, his friend sent all the necessary papers. And, so it was, with all kinds of preparations, they sent Barkev, at the age of eighteen, to this foreign country, the United States of America. Hripsime remembered the day well when he left. Everyone's emotions were high and it was hard to hold back the tears, but his excitement about what he wanted overruled any other emotion and they all became happy for him, including Hripsime. As they hugged one another and said their goodbyes, he promised he would return once he had his education.

When they moved to Beirut in 1956, Mihran was not able to do very much. Joel, George, and Aunt Lucy, who had now retired from being a kindergarten teacher, helped Hripsime pack everything; They were coming along to Beirut as well. Still, they left many of the bulky things behind. Finding a flat close to her daughter Marie and her husband, Henry, Beirut instantly stimulated Hripsime in a very pleasant and inspirational way. A grand place to live. All was very convenient. She could walk to all things including the downtown area. From their flat, they had a view of the waterfront and the tall hotels along the beach where tourists invaded the city all year round.

Joel and George continued to live with them as did Aunt Lucy. Mihran, because of his health was not able to evangelize as he once had, but he still would walk downtown to a street corner and hand out his evangelistic pamphlets. And, so they all enjoyed Beirut. Hripsime loved being near her daughter, husband, and grandsons Gilbert and Daniel. However, this grand arrangement did not last, because in the summer of 1965, Marie and her family moved to the States permanently. They stayed in Long Island for two years with Henry's sister while Henry went back to school and became certified as a physician in the States. Although he had been a physician in Beirut many years and had taken a one-year sabbatical at Iowa City Medical Center in 1957, he still had to complete many courses at an American university. Nothing was the same after this. And, when Hripsime would receive one of Marie's daily letters that told of her loneliness and how much she missed Beirut, this too did not help, as Hripsime missed them very much.

George also went with Marie and Henry and lived with them until he obtained a good job at Kennedy Airport in New York. He returned to Beirut to marry a woman named Miralda, but then returned and settled in New York for some time.

When Henry obtained his degree two years later in 1967, the family then moved to Omaha, Nebraska where he became a professor in microbiology.

In 1966, Joel also married a women named Miralda, and they had two sons, Raffi and Ara. They continued to live with

Hripsime and Mihran until they moved to West Beirut where Joel worked in a bank.

Barkev tried very hard, day and night to pay all of his expenses doing all sorts of very hard work for several years until he obtained his PhD from Harvard University in Boston. During this time, he became instantly attracted to a girl named Cathy who was working on her PhD, at the same university. The daughter of a well-known anthropologist, her degree was also in anthropology. When Barkev wrote Hripsime of their plans for marriage after they received their degrees, she was very happy for them. However, shortly before Barkev and Cathy were to be married, Mihran suffered two heart attacks. When they heard of this, they decided to come to Beirut for their honeymoon and to try and lift their spirits.

When they left to go back to the states, they told Hripsime and Mihran they were planning to settle in Tehran, Iran where they both had applied for positions at a university there. Hripsime was especially delighted at this news; Tehran was closer than the States. However, now she saw Mihran's illness as the beginning of many changes in her life and her once stable world began to crumble around her.

One day, while Mihran was passing out his pamphlets on his usual corner in downtown Beirut, a car ran over him. After much commotion, the driver of the car took Mihran to the nearest hospital, where he suffered a stroke. This caused a partial paralysis with little hope of recovery and his stay in the hospital was lengthy. When he finally did come home, he required a great deal of care and for twenty months Hripsime lovingly cared for him not knowing which day would be their last day together in this world.

Many friends came to visit Mihran during his last days. One friend told her, after he had passed on, that when he had asked

Mihran who was taking care of him, he responded, "My wife is taking good care of me. She is like my very own angel."

In 1967, before Mihran passed away to be with his precious Savior, Jesus Christ, whom he had served all of his life, many of Mihran's friends asked Hripsime to write about his life. Thinking a long time about this, she finally agreed, but asked them all to write their own testimonies about the special times they had with Mihran. With these testimonies, she added more of his personal life and told of some of his works, which culminated into a small book of one hundred and twenty-eight pages. When she had several hundred copies printed, she remembered the feeling of how inadequate this little book was, as Mihran's life was truly a blessed life. However, she felt no one could really tell of the inconceivable faith this man had in God and in his Savior and the works this faith produced in his life. At the funeral almost all the books were sold and Hripsime gave the money to an evangelical work that was one of Mihran's beloved ministries.

As Hripsime was lying on the floor, still rolled up in her blanket, she thought about this little book in more depth. It brought to mind many special memories of her dear husband. Then she recalled one particular time many years before their marriage, an astonishing experience he often talked about during their times together.

When Mihran was in the Turkish Army serving as a soldier during the First World War, he was an interpreter and a storekeeper for the Army's property. Many of the soldiers were jealous of him because of his high position in the army and because he was not involved in the fighting. One day, while Mihran was off duty, he went to a quiet place and sat with his Bible in his hands. He was meditating and praying when all of a sudden he saw the Commander-in-Chief walking toward him. Standing up at once, he saluted him in the military way.

As the commander came closer to him, he slapped him across his face very hard, and said to him, "Many are fighting and dying, and here you are having a nice time sitting and reading."

This was a great shock to Mihran for he felt he had not done any wrong against the army rule and for some time he could not calm down about the incident.

After a time, the same Commander came and said, in a very low and sorrowful tone, "My son, there has been a mistake. There was a complaint about another soldier, not about you."

In his own way, Mihran supposed the commander was telling him he was sorry, but the anger did not leave him immediately.

After he left, Mihran slipped down into his chair and while he tried to focus on what had just happened, Jesus came near to him in his heart and said to him, "My son, remember me, remember how I could bear so many slaps, mockings, beatings and how so many spit in my face. Can you not bear just one blow to your face, to your pride?"

Mihran felt so humiliated, he said, "Forgive me, my Lord Jesus, for not being able to bear one little slap."

As Mihran told Hripsime about how Jesus had comforted him with His loving presence, he said to her, "I have never been able to relay this experience adequately to anyone. This was not a dream," he explained to her. It was as if I were having an experience with a real person."

From that time on, as Mihran described it, his dedication to his Savior became a magnificent obsession. His teaching and preaching about Christ to others meant all things to him.

As more of Mihran's life shuffled through Hripsime's mind, another particular happening wedged itself into her thoughts and gloriously it came forth as a truly good example as to how things really were with Mihran.

On one unforgettable evening, about 9:30, Mihran had just put on his nightshirt, when she noticed he was taking it off again, and putting on his clothes once more.

Surprised, she asked him, "Where are you going at this late hour?"

"The Lord told me within my heart to go and visit someone who is in bed and to tell him about the salvation of his soul. Who knows, this may be his last chance to receive Jesus Christ as his personal Savior. Tomorrow it may be too late. I have to obey the Lord and give the message to him, the message that Jesus has shed His precious blood on the Cross of Calvary to wash away his sins. I must give him one more chance to invite Him into his heart," Mihran said, who was now fully dressed and standing in the open door.

As he closed the door behind him, Hripsime rolled over in bed and tried to sleep, but sleep did not come as she seemed only able to wait with open eyes for his return. When Mihran slipped back into the room an hour or so later, she could tell, it was with a cheerful heart.

When he realized Hripsime had been waiting for his return, he said, "It probably will not be until I am in Heaven that the result of this visit at such a late hour of the day will be revealed, but it is done and I know I have responded to God's will."

This was how Mihran was. He was always willing to go anytime, day or night, if he felt God was calling him. It was as if he had a direct line between himself and God.

Mihran's special interest was in the tract ministry. He used to translate interesting stories and have them printed into several languages: Armenian, Turkish with Armenian letters, English and

French and more. He was quite a linguist. He had knowledge of many languages: Armenian, Turkish, English, French, and German. When he first learned Turkish he used the Arabic alphabet, and, later, the Armenian alphabet. Therefore, because he knew the Arabic alphabet, when he was in his 60s and living in Beirut, he was able to teach himself to read the Arabic newspaper.

Anytime he went out, he would take many of these tracts and give them to anyone, as he was most assuredly led by the Lord. He would simply ask them if he or she would like to read it. Some would tear it up and throw it to the ground, but he never became disappointed. He carried this ministry until the last day of his life. He was giving out tracts at the time of the accident; however, this did keep him from handing out any more tracts the next two years. Nevertheless, he wrote and translated tracts, while he was in bed.

The last story he translated for a tract was about a preacher, the Reverend Jones and his wife. They had ventured to a new city to preach the Good News. On one of the first days after they had arrived, the Reverend and his wife started to visit some families and when they stopped in front of the first house they came to, he told his wife they should start with this house. When he knocked on the door and it opened, a man peeked through a hairline crack.

Without a smile, the man said, "What do you want?"

"Can we come in," Mrs. Jones said.

He was very rude and impolite, but could not seem to send them away. As they sat across from each other, the man sat in his chair repairing some old shoes. They later learned he was a cobbler. Reverend Jones stayed silent for several minutes and during his silence he prayed.

The man again asked rudely, "What is it you want?"

"We have come to see you," the Reverend Jones said, in a very friendly manner.

"Now you have seen me, so now you can go," the man replied.

"I am your new preacher and this is my wife. We want to have a friendly relationship with the families in the church. We have come to preach here and yours is the first house we came to."

"You don't know me. I am one who neither believes in God nor prays. I am the worst man in this town. My Name is John Brian. If you had heard about me, you would be so scared you would not stay here and be near me one more minute. So get out of my house as soon as possible," the man said.

"We have come to be a friend to you if you need one, but if you insist—Goodbye," the Reverend Jones said, as he grabbed his wife's hand and they headed for the door.

When they reached the street, the Reverend and his wife silently prayed for this man. Later, they learned that he was a famous atheist and blasphemer, known to all. He had never entered a church in all his life and indeed everybody was afraid of him.

Several weeks later, the little daughter of Reverend Jones entered her father's room. His shoes were in need of repair and he asked her if she would take his shoes to a cobbler.

"Which cobbler?" she said.

"Please take them to John Brian," the father said.

He decided he would show the cobbler some love and kindness even though he had been rude to them. He bound the shoes together and put a tract in one of them. The title of the tract was, *God Loves You—Jesus Died to Save You.*

After a week, the cobbler brought the shoes and gave them to the pastor who then paid him.

"Thank you very much for the pamphlet you put in your shoes," he said.

The Reverend Jones looked up in surprise as he had forgotten he had placed the tract in the shoes.

"That tract broke my heart. I wish you could visit me again and talk to me more about Jesus," he said.

Several months past and the cobbler developed an unbearable pain in his eyes. All the church people helped him in every way they could, but at last, he lost both of his eyes. However, now the eyes of his heart were open and he felt a real repentance of all his sins, whereby he invited Jesus Christ into his life and into his heart. He became a very powerful witness with a grand testimony to the forgiving power of the blood of Jesus that was shed on the Cross.

The congregation of the church became a great help to him financially and spiritually. Each time someone would come to visit him he would ask them to read a portion from the Bible. Each time that they did this, he would repeat these words, "I couldn't understand these words before I lost my eyes." Then he would praise the Lord for the joy of his salvation.

Sometimes the pastor's daughter, like a little angel, used to sit beside him and sing with her childish voice. He could not praise God enough for changing his whole life and for His promise of eternal life by means of a simple tract, a tract that had been put into the shoes that had been sent to him for repair. He passed away, but it was obvious to the whole of this church he went to be with his friend, Jesus.

Hripsime could hear her husband's voice now saying, "A timely spoken word or a tract given with a prayer behind it or one thrown onto a street corner or in front of a door may work wonders to break a hardened heart. This may be someone's only opportunity to receive Jesus Christ into their lives."

As she thought about how many had been blessed by reading these tracts, Hripsime thought about how Mihran would travel to different villages, towns or cities and preach the gospel or hand out his tracts. He would be away from home for several weeks and sometimes for months totally trusting the Lord for his finances.

When she would complain because he was away so often, he would say, "Half the reward is yours, Hripsime. As it is written in the Bible:

> For taking care of the children and keeping the
> home going in my absence, half the reward is
> yours. (I Samuel 30:24)

Near the end of Mihran's life, he told Hripsime, "You have to spend more time in the Lord's work. So far, you only have been busy with the housework and the children. After I pass on you will have more time to serve the Lord in any way you can."

As Hripsime thought about this, she realized that his wish had been fulfilled. A woman had asked her to guide a Bible study once a week in her home that was quite some distance. This lady would send a man to pick her up and take her back home. He was a very dear son of God and the Christian fellowship they experienced was very uplifting as he drove her back and forth to each meeting.

Praise God. This was a blessed opportunity to study the Word of God with others, she thought.

Also, this had helped her to feel closer to her late husband, as she now understood more about his ministry and why it had been important to be gone those long weeks and months.

A tear rolled down Hripsime's cheek as she thought about how God had prompted her marriage to Mihran and how well it had turned out. Closing her eyes, she slipped into a blissful sleep, as if she were in the arms of her Savior—Jesus.

— Nine —

The next day, the day of do or die, the day Shoushan's husband, Nerses was to come to pick her up, Hripsime prayed the whole time from the minute she awoke that morning to the minute he knocked on the door. When she opened it to see if it was indeed him, immediately, she saw the grave expression Nerses had on his face and knew his journey there must have been difficult and dangerous.

When Hripsime embraced him with much compassion, she spoke words that came from her heart saying, "Praise God that you are here." Opening the door wider, she asked, "Do you want to come in and sit a minute so you can rest?"

"No. It is best if we go now. We do not know what delays will be in store for us and we do not want to miss the boat. Are you ready?"

"Yes," she said, as she nodded at two bulging, medium-sized suitcases. One had a rope around the middle of it to keep it from popping open. These suitcases, as they were setting there in the middle of her empty flat, punched through her thoughts with the stark reality that somehow she had gotten her whole life into these two bundles.

As they descended the stairs, it seemed as if the darkness might swallow them up. It was as though they were descending into the bowels of the earth. Nerses held tightly onto her arm while he carried one of her suitcases and Hripsime carried the other. At the doorway that led to the street, a bullet pinged the casing of the door next to Hripsime's head. This caused them to pause for several seconds.

"Stay here until I can load these suitcases. I'll start the car, drive over here to you, and open the passenger door, so all you have to do is hop in. When I honk, keep low and move quickly."

As he grabbed the two suitcases and scurried toward the car with his heavy burdens, Hripsime prayed silently and asked the Lord for his protection. Although bullets were flying in every direction, he made it to the car. Squeezing the suitcases into the trunk, he motioned for Hripsime to get ready. Slamming the lid, he continued in a crouched position and rounded the car. Hripsime said thank you to God, as he slid into the driver's seat.

The car made a squealing u-turn and was now directly in front of her only a few paces away. The passenger door was open and she heard the beep of the horn. Looking all around her, she leaped across the sidewalk. She could hear words coming from the car, "Run, Hripsime, get in the car! Quick!"

Miraculously, they were now both inside the car. The car lurched forward, but it was a slow bumpy ride through the narrow streets between the shelled-out buildings. Filled with rubble and burning cars, sometimes no real impasse existed and a detour was necessary down a side street. This rubble and debris jostled the car about and Hripsime had to hold on tightly, not only to the dash, but to the back of the seat. Once she hit her head on the ceiling of the car and then on the windshield, as the car rolled over an enormous block of cement. Pieces of rebar stuck out of it in every direction. Hripsime could imagine it puncturing the tires, but this did not happen.

Now they were in the inner city where the buildings were taller and the streets were more even and there seemed to be more of a pathway. Able to take in more clearly the scenery outside the car, she was horrified at the destruction all around them. Many buildings had collapsed. Many, some as tall as ten stories, were empty shells tilting toward the street. Layers of jagged shards, piles of crumbled cement and debris hampered all progress no matter whether a person was walking or driving. Some piles were as tall as a one-story building. Pillars of smoke from isolated small fires reached above the buildings and into the gray-black skies above.

Now bullets haphazardly crossed in the path of the car, which caused them to have to zigzag down a dubious pathway. Hripsime remembered when this was once a grand avenue. Then finally, they pulled up in front of her niece's building, but the car was on the opposite side of the street.

"It looks like this is the closest we can park," her nephew-in-law said, in a tone that said he was deeply worried.

"Your building has so much damage and there are so many bombed out cars here. You must have had it very rough," Hripsime sympathized.

"Yes. And, the smell is very nauseous at times even inside our building. Some things have been burning for days," he said, as his voice trailed off full of discouragement.

Silently, they looked at one another. Silently, Hripsime praised God they had gotten this far in their perilous flight.

"Maybe you should wait here while I go get Shoushan."

"No, I cannot stay here alone. No, I'll go with you and help carry things."

"Someone is watching most of our belongings on the beach. We only have a few things to take with us now."

"No, I'll go with you."

If Mihran would have been there, she would not have been so afraid, but as it was, her faith seemed to be waning at that moment, as a bullet now cracked the side window near her. Both of them jumped from the car simultaneously, and both ran neck-and-neck toward the building. Crouched low, heads ducked, with hands covering their heads, it reminded Hripsime of waddling ducks fresh out of water. As they went along, Hripsime not only heard the bullets flying overhead she could feel them as they whistled by her. Once inside the entryway, they paused to catch their breath. Then the front door opened and Hripsime's niece came running up to her and hugged her dearly.

"Thank you dear one for coming to get me," Hripsime said, with a shaky voice.

"I love you, Auntie. We had to bring you with us," she said, as she again hugged Hripsime with one of the warmest biggest smiles.

"We must move along," her husband urged, motioning with his hands.

After a few more words, they ran up the stairs to their flat on the second floor and hurriedly snatched up the suitcases that were bunched together in a pile by the door. Rushing back down the stairs, Hripsime brought up the rear with a lot less agility than the younger ones. It seemed to her they were bouncing down the stairs toward the street with the resiliency of rubber beach balls; nothing seemed to tire them. The trio hesitated for several minutes in the entryway, as they looked out at the car on the other side of the road. It seemed a very great distance to Hripsime. As she took some deep breaths of smoky air, again she prayed silently that God would spread his protective wings around them on this last leg of their precarious journey. She also asked Him to give her the strength she needed to do what she had to do.

Finally, with their arms full, they took one last look at one another and ran, one after the other in a parade-like procession. Bullets pinged and whistled through the air all around them. By the grace of God alone, they reached the car without a bullet hitting any of them. Throwing the luggage into the back seat, sandwiching themselves into the front seat, they slammed the doors at the same time of the two-door sedan. Hripsime began to feel somewhat safe, that is until a bullet ricocheted off the back window. It left a hole that eventually shattered it. Still, what was important, the car was moving and they were heading for the seashore. As they approached the sandy beach, the shooting diminished, and then it stopped altogether. Eventually, all war-like sounds were distant; seemingly they were away from any serious skirmishes or sharp shooters.

We have escaped. Thank you my merciful Father, Hripsime sighed.

She kept her comment inside of her though, as they would not understand that she could feel God's presence with them and He was telling her that everything was going to be fine.

"I am here," He said, as plainly as if He were sitting next to her.

Although it was late in the afternoon, the sun was burning hot. As they stood waiting for their names to be called among a big crowd of smelly, dripping-wet bodies, Hripsime noticed there were many like themselves, a wave of people along the beach. All were waiting patiently. All eyes were staring out at the piers that held the all too few boats. When a family name rang out, small individual bands, laden with bags and boxes, would lunge forward from the mass, and then stumble up onto one of the long piers that jutted out into the harbor. Looking intently for the name of their precious boat, no one relaxed, not for even an instant. The anxiety and anticipation that filled the air was so intense, a knife could have cut through it.

At last, they heard their names called and then another few names were called. Oh, what a sight it was! They were among several families as they pushed, pulled and rushed onto the pier and onto their assigned boat.

At last, settled inside a very small cabin with little space to stretch their tired legs, Hripsime was able to look out one of the small portals. What she saw saddened her greatly. Many were still waiting on the beach in the torrid heat, far too many, and the sun was setting. She felt extremely grateful, as they seemed to be one of the more fortunate groups.

Hripsime suddenly felt very tired. The day had caught up to her. Besides what it took to get there, they had been standing several hours on the seashore under the hot sun. She kept peering out the tiny portal and watching the sun as it sank into the sea. She felt as if she were sinking along with it.

The night was a very long night. By airplane, it would have taken half an hour from Beirut to Cyprus, but by boat it took sixteen hours, which seemed more like sixty. On that particular night, there was a horrible storm on the Mediterranean. During the entire voyage, the high tides and high winds tossed the boat without mercy. Her niece was very sick and she spent most of the night and the next morning curled up in a ball in the corner with a basin next to her head. Her husband would run to empty it down the narrow rocking corridor every now and then. Hripsime lay there with her eyes open as she tried to keep herself in the confines of the bunk. The sickness wanted to come, but she kept her mind focused elsewhere—she kept it focused on Jesus.

When they arrived in Cyprus, people were on top of people. They could barely make a path through the waves of humanity. Every nook and cranny available was taken. This incredible sight caused Hripsime much dismay as they went along and realized the entire city was crowded beyond capacity. Many of the people embarking from the many boats from Beirut had to settle on street corners and alley ways, because all of the hotels, churches, schools and hotels were full. This was a time when many Christians were fleeing Beirut every day. Fortunately, Nersus' brother lived in Cyprus and after they reached his house and were safely settled in, Hripsime silently praised God for saving them from certain death and for giving them this safe place to stay when so many did not have a place to lay their head.

The next business was to cable Barkev and Cathy in Tehran, Iran and tell them of their escape.

A student slipped Cathy the cable while she was lecturing to her class at the university. Taking a minute to read it, she looked up at her class and told her students, "This is an emergency. I must go right away. You are dismissed."

Cathy then hurried to the American Embassy in Tehran and tried to obtain a visa for Cyprus, but was told that it was impossible to procure one from Iran to Cyprus. Giving the matter more thought, she decided to go then to Israel. Flying to Israel, she finally obtained a visa to Cyprus. She then cabled Hripsime and informed her as to which plane she would be arriving on and they met her at the airport in Cyprus.

When Cathy came down the ramp into the waiting area, they embraced with such love and affection for one another that Hripsime momentarily was overcome. As they walked along the concourse, four-wide abuzz, Cathy explained how difficult it had been to gather the visas, but that everything had worked out in an incredible way. Hripsime silently thanked God as her niece and her husband relayed to Cathy the horrors of their escape from Beirut.

After it became the goal that Hripsime was to live with Marie in the States, the way everything worked together for her to go there was indeed another miracle. Cathy had scheduled a flight earlier to California for a special project for her university in Tehran. And, as it turned out, the date and timing could not have been more perfect if the two of them had sat down and planned it from the beginning. If she had gone one day earlier or one day later, it would have been impossible for Hripsime to travel with her. Hripsime was deeply thankful for this for she could not imagine traveling alone to America. Within itself, it was something she had never dreamt was possible. Deeply entrenched in her own world in Beirut, this was all she had ever known. Always she had been stubborn when asked to stay with one of her children. The thought of dependency charged at her like a wild boar. And the thought of living in a different country, well, it was all she could do to move from Aleppo to Beirut twenty years before, and that was when steadfast Mihran was with her.

From Cyprus, a stopover in Athens for one night was necessary and then the next day they flew on to Tehran. During this time, hard decisions were made. As she was saying her goodbyes to Barkev and Joel and their families, it was difficult for her to imagine life in America.

Maybe, she thought, *maybe Iran would do just fine.*

However, Marie and Henry and her grand-children were waiting in Nebraska and she was anxious to see George and his wife, Miralda, as they were still living in New York at this time.

From Tehran, Cathy and Hripsime flew into Kennedy Airport in New York where George and Miralda anxiously awaited their arrival. It was a wonderful visit before Cathy had to fly from Long Island to California. When they said their goodbyes at the airport, Hripsime could not thank her enough for what she had done: retrieving her from Cyprus and bringing her to America. Silently, while she waved to Cathy, who was waving and blowing kisses as she walked into the narrow tunnel that led to her plane, she thanked God for the many miracles that had made it all possible for her to come to America. God surely had planned every detail.

As she watched Cathy's huge plane pull away from the terminal and taxi to the runway, Hripsime prayed resolutely that Cathy and Barkev and all those dear to her, would draw closer to the Lord. She thanked Him for how his hand was obviously upon her whole family.

When Hripsime awoke to the fact that Cathy was gone and she was again alone, she became fearful once more. Ever since her trip to Addis-Abba, she never wanted to fly alone again. She now prayed that she would not have to fly this last leg of the trip by herself. Then it came about that Gilbert, Marie and Henry's first son would be with her on the plane from New York to Omaha.

Gilbert had been a young teen, only fifteen years when the family left Beirut in 1965. She learned he was now an electrical engineer working for a large electronics manufacturer and had been assigned to a project in Russia. He had become ill and was taking some sick leave to go home and get well. Just at the right time he was on the same plane and was now accompanying his grandmother to Omaha. This gave Hripsime the confidence that this was where God wanted her to be. When they arrived unharmed in Omaha in the loving arms of Henry and Marie, who embraced her as if she had never been gone from their sight, again she knew this must be where God wanted her.

The excitement was indeed wonderful, but still something was unsettling to her soul. Something nagged at her and tugged at her heart, but she did not know what it was.

That same evening, when Hripsime was alone in her new bed, she could not relax, the pillows were too soft, the covers to posh, and the mattress too comfortable. Then she tried to think through how all of it was possible, how she could now be in America. She had been only a simple, little, orphan girl, abandoned in a boarding school in Marash. She had survived the life and death struggles of the French and Turkish War, and she had obtained an advanced education, something unheard of for an orphan and for a woman of those times. She had married an educated and spiritual man of God and had borne four beautiful children. She had endured the Second World War in Aleppo and now she had survived the Lebanese Civil War where she had endured terrible fighting day and night. And now, the biggest miracle of them all, she had arrived in the United States and was now at her dear daughter's home in Nebraska.

Yes, it all must be considered one miracle after another and for God's purpose, she thought. *Why else would these miracles have happened to her?*

She knew that most likely she would never really know the reason, but she tried to learn how to become more satisfied within her soul about it all. As the months went by and then the years Hripsime still could not shake off the feeling of estrangement that plagued her. Although there were happy times: Dan and Debra Ann's wedding and the birth of her two great grandchildren, Armen and Leah, she had a restless spirit within her.

One Sunday afternoon when a slight breeze rustled the tree tops and the family was strolling along a pathway at Omaha's Henry Doorly Zoo, Hripsime and Marie happened to be walking along by themselves.

"Mother, sometimes I get the feeling you are not happy," Marie said.

"I feel like I don't fit in with all of you," Hripsime responded.

"You don't like being with us?"

"I truly love being with you and your family. I love you all very much. But,…I miss my long strolls to downtown Beirut, that cup of coffee at one of the sidewalk cafes, and my friends there who understood the depth of life we had all experienced," she repined. There is too much complacency here, Marie, although I do understood how easy it is for someone to feel safe within the boundaries of America; this country does seem isolated. However, I find this country's blasé ways hard to understand, hard to accept."

Hripsime bit her lip as she said these things and realized that maybe she was saying too much.

Marie looked at her a minute as if she was trying to understand, but then responded, "I know mother. This was my problem too when I first moved here. I tried to write you about it when we were in New York, but it is hard to explain. All I can say to you is I know what you are feeling. It is a very different culture here."

"No fault can be placed on anything or anyone, however, something keeps inwardly pulling at me and saying that a time will come when America can no longer escape from the terrible terrors that dominate the other parts of this world. I find myself often praying about the spiritually of those I meet. I fear someday it will be too late for some of these people. Marie, there are so many who do not know Him. There is no other way to ward off such fears; God, through his son Jesus Christ is the only answer, Marie. As you know, Jesus says,

> I am the way, the truth and the life: no man
> cometh unto to the Father, but by me. (John 14:6)

"Yes. Yes, mother. If only all could see. I believe there will be perfect harmony in this world when Jesus returns, just as he has promised."

"Yes. Although you and your brothers, Joel, George and Barkev, know Him and have known him since childhood, there may be some in our family that don't, especially those in future generations. My heart aches for these things, especially when I think of Gilbert, Dan and Debra Ann and their little ones, Armen and Leah. Please push the Bible and your father's ways into their lives and pray for them after I am gone, Marie."

"I will," Marie said. "You know my heart aches in the same way and that I pray every day that everyone in our family will draw closer to Him."

"Thank you, Jesus. Marie, I am thankful I am alive after the wars and hardships I have been through and to see all that I am seeing now, but I am most thankful that I am alive in Christ. He is the only true protection and comfort in a world where so much evil thrives. Your father was right. I did not see it then as much as I see it now. Suddenly, I understand more about the urgency Mihran felt for those who do not have Christ. Oh, Marie let's stop here on this park bench and pray for those in our family who may not have the salvation and for the future generations in our family," Hripsime said, as she pulled Marie by her arm and they headed for a nearby empty bench with an urgency Hripsime did not even understand.

"Oh, Heavenly Father, we lift each one up to you in this family who does not know You. And, there's Luther and his family too. Bring them to You before it is too late. We thank you Father for the way You have brought me through so much and that each generation is being blessed now, but we pray now they will all be drawn even closer to You and that all will be done for Your Glory and Praise. I will never be able to thank you enough, Lord, for how Your hand has been on each one of us all these years. And I pray for the little ones I see now and for those who are not yet born that don't know or will know the ways on the other side of this world. Please, my Father, protect them and keep them in Your loving arms and draw them one and all to You. Thank you for the hope we have in your promise.

> And the Lord thy God will circumcise thine heart,
> and the heart of thy seed, to love the Lord thy God
> with all thine heart, and with all thy soul, that thou
> mayest live. (Deut. 30:6)

Then God lifted this burden from Hripsime's soul and she felt suddenly at peace, as she and Marie clutched their hands together more tightly and they embraced one another as if it were their last time together.

"I love you, Marie. I thank God for you every day," Hripsime said, with a tear in her eye. The Bible studies you are leading in the homes of others remind me so much of your father."

"This reminds me more of you, mother."

"But it was your father who always prompted such things?"

"Yes, I remember, mother. I remember well my 'Hairig' (Armenian for daddy) and his wonderful faith. I remember how he and Aunt Lucy and you shared with us continually the Bible, His holy and living word, and how we all memorized Bible passages, and how each of you always reminded us of how much Jesus loved us. I remember how he always had a smile and the joy of the Lord was always with him in spite of circumstances. I remember how you, Hairig and Aunt Lucy would always pray for us, and with us, and how little by little we learned.

"Remember, mother, when Dad would be praying and we would all be around him. Supposedly, we were to keep our eyes closed, but I thought if I peeked I could see who he was praying to. God, his Lord and Savior was always so very real to Him, and I wanted so to see Him as he saw Him. I remember most of all when he went to be with the Lord. We all knew he loved and worshiped and trusted and served Him, and so we knew where he was, but I have missed him so very much, mother."

"Yes. You were his little girl."

Neither said anything for a few minutes. Then Hripsime added, "Promise me Marie you will continue always with the Bible studies. He always wanted me to reach out to others in some way and I know this would have pleased him very much to know you are teaching His word."

"Of course, mother. This is always on my heart."

Just at that moment Henry and the others were upon them and then they were pulling them up off the bench and toward the cage where the lions were lounging in the sun.

On another day, while she was watching her great grandchildren playing, a thought came to Hripsime. The family had gathered for a picnic, a family reunion of sorts. George and his wife, Miralda were there from New York and Gilbert had returned again from Russia. The two great grandchildren, the shinning lights of the gathering, were throwing a ball to one another. Leah beamed as she looked over at her great grandmother and threw it to Armen. Armen was now carrying it toward a make-shift goalpost. His little legs were going as fast they could with the ball tucked under his arm pit. Proudly he looked over his shoulder at Hripsime. The others were chasing him down and gaining quickly, but steadily he kept running. Marie came up from behind and laid her hand on Hripsime's shoulder as they watched together.

"Marie," Hripsime suddenly said, "I have noticed that you love your children more. Your love is more apparent and more instinctive than mine was for you and your brothers."

Marie looked at Hripsime with a great deal of concern and said, "What on earth are you talking about, mother?"

"About how we love our children differently. I am sure some of this comes from being abandoned by my parents who were taken away in the deportation when I was very young and the things I saw at Marash before I met your father, but I want you to know I love you very much, Marie. Some day I hope you will meet Luther and his family and especially his daughter who made it possible for me to be here. Although we went through the same plight, his experience seemed more astonishing than mine. Still, the abrupt way our parents and family were taken from us when we were so young surely must have affected us. And, the horrors at Marash that I witnessed; I know these things have caused me to be indifferent in some ways and not as loving as I could be."

"Mother, I think I understand."

"I know it is hard for anyone to understand who has not seen these evil things with their own eyes. Sometimes I ponder, Marie, how much the soul can bear before it becomes too hard and we cannot love at all."

"But, mother, you are born again. Your love is now God's love."

"Yes. You're right. I know God's love flows through me to those that he is trying to reach. And it is a far better love, a true and genuine love that comes from God."

"It's a forgiving love, an unconditional love, a complete love," Marie added.

"Yes," Hripsime said, as she contemplated all of this."

"Isn't this a wonderful thing that no matter what we have been through Jesus heals and loves others through us."

Hripsime had to admit there was a great deal of insight in her daughter's wisdom, but still she felt confused about this and so she answered, "Yes, but maybe it is impossible to heal a soul completely that has seen too much?"

"I think not, mother. I am very proud you are my mother. And, as for loving me, you must admit, I did not turn out all that bad."

They now hugged one another in a deep embrace and it was hard to let go.

"You are right, my daughter, my dear one. You did not turn out all that bad. You are very loving."

"Thank you, Lord."

That afternoon Hripsime went off away from the others and found a quiet spot in the orchard. She knelt down under a large apple tree and prayed as she had never prayed before. She prayed that God would wipe away all the old scars from her past that He would wipe the slate clean as she released it and gave it to Him. Again, Mihran's words filled her thoughts about total trust, and she knew this was the answer and the key to loving others.

When she asked God to help her with this new commitment, miraculously, her demeanor changed overnight. She found she had more compassion than she had ever had before. She found herself rapt up more tightly in her children and grand-children and especially her two little great-grandchildren. And, she seemed to find time, more than before, to read God's promises to them.

Hripsime had been living with Marie and Henry and their family now for eight years with no visible signs of poor health, but in January of 1985 when Hripsime was probably somewhere in her eighties, the Lord took her quietly in her sleep.

It was on the night of the first birthday party she had ever had. All the children, grandchildren and great-grandchildren had proclaimed this day Hripsime's birthday and a grand time was had by all that entire day. However, when the sun set and evening came and Hripsime blew out the single candle on her cake, she knew somehow that this was not only her first birthday party, but her last. After she kissed each one goodnight, she wearily climbed the stairs to her bedroom. Slipping into her long nightgown that rustled along the floor, she opened the window a crack to let in a fresh, snowy breeze and the winter smell of evergreen before she slid between the sheets, blankets and the puffy comforter. After she switched the bedside lamp off, she laid her head on the soft pillows, something she still had not quite gotten used to. She thanked God for the wonderful day, as she ran it through her mind scene by scene.

Briefly, she thought about the deportation and how her parents and family had suffered; about how the Armenians had faced extinction, but yet she had survived; and about her wonderful family now and especially those that were alive in Him.

And she thought, *the enemy could not kill all of us.*

She now remembered a scripture in Romans that comforted her to the highest degree.

> Nay, in all these things we are more than conquerors through him that loved us. For I am persuaded...our Lord. (Romans 8:37-39)

Then she thought of how God had singled her out, as He had her brother, and how He had caused all this good to come from the bad. This may have been part of some kind of master plan of His, but who can fathom what God knows or does.

"Thank you, Jesus," she softly whispered into the darkness. "For whatever the reason you spared me above everyone else, I thank you. And, I thank you for my family and the heritage that can never be taken from them."

This now caused her mind to dwell on yet another verse in Romans:

> And we know that all things work together for good to them that love God, to them who are the called according to His purpose. (Romans 8:28)

As she meditated on this most important verse, she then thought of another.

> Thy kingdom is an everlasting kingdom, and thy dominion endureth throughout all generations. (Psalms 145:13)

Before she closed her eyes, she noticed an image at the foot of her bed. At first it was faint, but then it became clearer. In a long white robe, she recognized Mihran. A glowing light encircled him. A warm feeling waved through her whole body as she took in the glowing image of her dear husband. Then two more images appeared at the end of her bed. Their white robes draped dramatically to the floor as well and their faces glowed with an inner light that was bedazzling. Or was this her imagination? Yet, they had a presence that reminded Hripsime of her mother and her father.

Now her eyes grew heavy and soon they closed, but not before a sweet smile spread across her face. Jesus was on her mind and an unexplainable love welled up inside of her to the fullest. Suddenly, a sharp breeze pushed its way through the crack in the window and swirled about the darkened room, but then, all at once, the room was silent, except for the sound of the wind whistling through the pines outside Hripsime's window. At the same time of Hripsime's last breath, the pines softly succumbed as well, but soon the snowy, icy Nebraska storm raged on, one that was very similar to a snowy, icy storm long ago in Zeitoun, Turkey.

Epilogue

As I can imagine it, as I see her looking down on the situation as it is this day, I believe Hripsime would agree with me that the turmoil and strife she predicted has indeed happened. I also believe Hripsime would be amazed at the phenomenal way the Gospel is being translated into every language and is reaching every nook and cranny throughout the world. Even the most unlikely are noticing, as many Muslim terrorists now are proclaiming the name of Jesus in their hearts.

My prayer is that Hripsime's prayer may become a reality in everyone's life who reads her miraculous story, and may God lift your faith, as He has mine. May all honor and glory be to God the Father through his Son, Jesus Christ.

> For the earth is the Lord's and everything in it,…for he founded it upon the seas and established it upon the waters.
> (Psalm 24:1,2)

For God so loved the world that he gave his one and only Son, that whoever believes in him shall not perish but have eternal life. For God did not send his Son into the world to condemn the world, but to save the world through him. (John 3:16,17)

For the grace of God that brings salvation has appeared to all men. It teaches us to say "No" to ungodliness and worldly passions, and to live self-controlled, upright and godly lives in this present age, while we wait for the blessed hope – the glorious appearing of our great God and Savior, Jesus Christ, who gave himself for us to redeem us from all wickedness and to purify for himself a people that are his very own, eager to do what is good. (Titus 2:11-14)

For Jesus answered: "I am the way and the truth and the life. No one comes to the Father except through me. If you really know me, you would know my Father as well." (John 14:6).

Come to me, all you who are weary and burdened, and I will give you rest. Take my yoke upon you and learn from me, for I am gentle and humble in heart, and you will find rest for your souls. For my yoke is easy and my burden is light. (Matthew 11:28-30);

Dear friends, let us love one another, for love comes from God. Everyone who loves has been born of God and knows God. Whoever does not love does not know God, because God is love.…This is love: not that we loved God, but that He loved us and sent his Son as an atoning sacrifice for our sins… God is love. Whoever lives in love lives in God, and God in him. (I John 4: 7-10, 16)

"Blessed are the peacemakers, for they will be called sons of God." (Matthew 5:9)